Management in Post-Mao China
An Insider's View

Research for Business Decisions, No. 76

Richard N. Farmer, Series Editor

Professor of International Business
Indiana University

Other Titles in This Series

Management in Post-Mao China
An Insider's View

by
Joseph Y. Battat

School of Business
Indiana University

UMI RESEARCH PRESS
Ann Arbor, Michigan

Produced and distributed by
UMI Research Press
an imprint of
University Microfilms, Inc.
Ann Arbor, Michigan 48106

Library of Congress Cataloging in Publication Data

Battat, Joseph Y.
  Management in post-Mao China.

  (Research for business decisions ; no. 76)
  Includes bibliographical references and index.
  1. Management—China. I. Title. II. Series.
HD70.C5B38   1986   658'.00951   86-6957
ISBN 0-8357-1663-5 (alk. paper)

To the Chinese people,
a source of
inspiration and learning

Contents

Figures

Preface

In a fatalistic mood one might say that this book is the result of chance: my being in the right place at the right time. The Chinese curse "May you live in interesting times" did not apply to me. I was fortunate to experience living in a society just when the traumatic ten-year-long Cultural Revolution had ended and the country was poised at a crossroads where its fate was to be decided. The whole Chinese society was experiencing the kind of emotional storm that wraps and grasps an individual immediately following the end of a painful, costly personal tragedy. One minute he is full of hope, ready to take full advantage of life to recover lost time and take revenge over his ugly past fate; the next minute he is apprehensive about what the future may hold, about the fragility of the just recovered normality of life. His memory is still full of the cruel time he has experienced, and he keeps asking himself: "Have things changed, after all?" He is constantly monitoring and analyzing signals, hoping to find a positive answer to this question to strengthen his hopes.

I lived in China for two and one-half years during fascinating times, soon after the death of Mao Ze-dong, and at the time when the course of post-Mao China was being charted. The whole society was recovering emotionally and physically from the trauma of the Cultural Revolution. It was in a state of flux, indecisiveness, confusion, transition and experimentation. For most of my stay in China, I worked inside Chinese organizations as their employee, and thus was able to observe developments closely.

Thanks to my firsthand observations and involvement as an agent of change, I was in a position to capture the dynamics of those changes both at the macro level and, more fascinating and unusual for foreigners, at the micro level. In addition to facts and hard data traditionally used in studies like this one, a flavor of the general mood and atmosphere prevalent in China is offered particularly through the case studies. To take advantage of the uniqueness of the data at a time when foreigners' access to the workings of Chinese organizations was extremely limited, and to give the data ample space for presentation, this book focuses on selective developments within the fields of economies and management for the period spanning mid-1977 to early 1980. It acts as a linchpin between management practices in late Mao China and in the 1980s, and sheds light on management studies covering recent years.

This book is addressed foremost to two groups of readers: people currently working or who may work inside Chinese organizations, and who would greatly benefit from an insight into Chinese management practices; and observers and students of post-Mao China's economic and management reforms. To broaden their perspective, students of the economic development of developing countries and of economic and management reforms of centrally planned economies will find this book useful. Finally, sections of this study are of benefit to observers of the management of the transfer of technology and of the development of management education, both as parts of modernization efforts in a developing country setting.

Chapters 1 and 2 briefly describe early developments of post-Mao economic and enterprise management systems against official policy pronouncements and the general post-Cultural Revolution context. From the macro level, the study moves to the micro level. We enter Chinese organizations to observe their management of two activities directly related to the most recent reforms: the revival of management education and the transfer of high technology. Chapters 4 and 5 give detailed descriptions of post-Mao China's earliest serious efforts in those two areas, presenting developments at the national level as well as particular cases. An analysis of Chinese management is offered in chapter 6.

Keeping in mind the official pronouncements concerning change and shift in policies as described in the macro level analysis of the first part of this study, one finds when observing and analyzing the micro level both divergence and congruence in the two levels. Congruence is reflected in the organization's sharing of the views, values and needs stated in the pronouncements of the central authorities, in new policy formulation and implementation, as well as in positive response to policy shifts and new requirements. The divergence stems from both subjective and objective factors that exist within the organization, and the environment it was facing. If the observed organizations are considered as a microcosm of the rest of the nation, or simply as representatives of similar organizations in China, a study of such congruence and divergence would help formulate a preliminary assessment of the environment within which the new policies were being implemented, and speculate as to the relative importance of a number of factors affecting the degree of success or failure of those policies.

In other words, to what extent will the policy shifts change China in this "new historical period," as the current leadership likes to call the post-Mao era, and to what extent will it not? Also, what could the rate of change be?

Here, we must introduce the concept of change and continuity as it applies to the case of China. It is wrong to say that there has been no change in China in the thirty years since the Communist Party came to national power. The country possesses a new political, economic and social system. Its level and direction of economic development are undoubtedly different from the ones under the Guomindang regime of Chiang Kai-chek. Today's arts and literature in China reflect both the country's traditional heritage and new socialist values and aesthetics.

Yet to say that the People's Republic of China has no common ground with "old China" would be equally wrong. Notwithstanding the implantation of socialist values, traditional values are alive and well in the People's Republic, as demonstrated by the failure of the Cultural Revolution and by current policies. The national economy is basically agrarian, in terms of the size of the contribution of the agricultural sector to the gross national product, and of the rural population. Notwithstanding the graft of socialism it received, China's political culture remains basically the same. Thus, one must examine China in terms of the interplay of continuity and change, and should not discount the powerful forces of either. For example, Mao Ze-dong had made an insightful and probably correct analysis of the social and political forces before coming to national power, and was able to muster and direct some of them successfully. Yet, his penchant for socialist romanticism and impatience in introducing changes into "New China" led to mixed results, at best. He clearly did not succeed in creating the "new Chinese," imbued with Mao's views and the values of the "communist man," nor in implementing the policies of the Great Leap Forward and the Cultural Revolution. Mao's underestimation of the forces of continuity has led to the demise of some of his policies and to great sufferings by the Chinese people.

The research method used in this study is participant observation, which is discussed in chapter 3. It is, however, necessary to mention here that data for this research have been collected through my direct participation in the work of Chinese organizations; the numerous discussions I held with colleagues, friends, teachers, students, "the man on the street," and government officials; and materials I have collected while in China.

Materials in all chapters focus on the period spanning mid-1977 to the end of 1979. In rare cases, such as in the chapter on management education, data collected in a subsequent visit to China in 1980 are added. When helpful to the understanding of the impact of policies, decisions and actions taken during the period covered in the study, mention is made of developments that took place in 1980 and 1981.

Both in the tradition of Western ways of treating sources of data, and to respect the explicit or implicit desires for anonymity of my data sources, these sources remain confidential, unless otherwise appropriate. In such cases, the sources of data will be referred to as "personal notes."

All translations of Chinese texts or conversations are original, and made by me, unless otherwise indicated. Also, the Pinyin transliteration of Chinese is used throughout the text.

Acknowledgments

This study would not have been possible without the full help and support of many Chinese people, who held hours of discussions with me and provided valuable information. I was privileged to have been given the opportunity to work for an extended period of time inside Chinese organizations, to take part in their decision-making process, and, at times, to represent them abroad and in China. I was honored to be the recipient of their trust and confidence. Whatever benefit this research may offer Chinese readers, it can never match the wealth of knowledge I gained from the Chinese people, to whom this study is dedicated.

Richard D. Robinson has given me his strong encouragement and full support since the inception of this study. His contribution is but the latest in a series that has spanned over a decade. He has been my mentor and a source of inspiration, and has instilled in me an *esprit critique*. Dwight H. Perkins and John VanMaanen offered advice on research design, content, form and methodology, all of which have substantially enhanced the quality of this study. Finally, my thanks to Dr. Margaret Lourie for her able editorial support. To all of these individuals, I am gratefully indebted.

The Institute of Current World Affairs generously provided financial and material support during my work on the first part of the study, following an earlier fellowship, in the mid-1970s, which helped me learn about China and its people, prior to my living there. The East Asian Studies Center and the Research Institute For Inner Asian Studies at Indiana University graciously offered me their facilities to finish my research. To all these organizations, I express my thanks.

No words, however couched, can adequately express my deepest gratitude to a woman who, as a true life companion, has shared my ups and downs; who has greatly contributed, perhaps unknowingly, to this study through her advice and comments; who graciously put in long hours of editing; who has untiringly coached me in the language of Shakespeare for 15 years; and who did not hesitate to bear all sorts of sacrifices to see this study completed. I also thank my two children for the understanding that they showed, despite their young age, as to why I stayed away from them so much.

1

Post-Mao Developments in
Economic Policies (1977–80)

The first scene of the last act of the political power struggle in post-Mao China began on September 9, 1976, the day Mao Ze-dong died. It took close to five years for the dénouement to unfold at the Sixth Plenary Session of the Central Committee of the Eleventh Party Congress held in Beijing in June 1981. That session approved the new leadership, thus placing the center of power for both the Chinese Communist Party and the Chinese government with people who leaned towards Deng Xiao-ping's political views. This new leadership wanted to see the country embark on a course of rapid, sustained, yet orderly economic development, the direction and policies of which had been carefully and painstakingly set during the previous five years.

This chapter briefly traces developments in post-Mao China in a number of areas—political, social, economic and educational. In most cases, I follow a chronological presentation, using political developments as the point of departure.

The New Political Scene

There seems to be a year of pivotal significance in the history of a country. One such year in the People's Republic of China was 1976, when a number of events set the stage for a new era in its recent history.

Best known of the events were the deaths of three top Chinese leaders, all over 70 years old. In January, Zhou En-lai, vice-chairman of the Chinese Communist Party and premier of the government, passed away. He had been an active leader in the party and its army since their foundation. Until his death, he had been the one and only premier since the government's establishment in 1949. In that capacity, he had taken an active part in the country's political, cultural, economic and social life. His leadership record and style won him the deep respect of much of the Chinese population.

In July, Zhu De died. He was to many Chinese the "father of the People's Liberation Army." Indeed, his contributions to the establishment and development of the communist armed forces and to their operational successes, particularly before

1949, were widely recognized. However, unlike both Mao Ze-dong and Zhou En-lai, he was no longer at the center of power at the time of his death.

In September, the death of Mao Ze-dong, a towering though controversial figure of the Chinese revolution, brought an end to an era in China's history. Since 1935, Mao had been the undisputed head of the communist leadership that successfully fought for power and had ruled the country since 1949. As expected, his death brought the power struggle to new heights, yet closer to its conclusion.

Also for political reasons, 1976 was a landmark year in the history of the People's Republic of China. For the first time since 1949, against the will and power of the authorities, large-scale grass-root demonstrations erupted in early April in a number of urban areas, notably Beijing and Nanjing. For instance, in what is known as "The Tian An Men Incident," more than a million people from all walks of life gave vent to their political feelings in Beijing's Tian An Men Square over Qingming Day.[1] They were expressing their strong dissatisfaction with many of the Cultural Revolution's policies, with the leaders that supported those policies,[2] and with the posthumous attacks that were launched against Zhou En-lai and the policies for which he stood.[3]

Four weeks after the death of Mao Ze-dong in September 1976 came the removal of the Gang of Four, which included Jiang Qing, Mao's widow; Zhang Qun-qiao, vice-chairman of the Chinese Communist Party and vice-premier; Wang Hong-wen, vice-chairman of the Chinese Communist Party; and Yao Wen-yuan, a propagandist. All were members of the Party's powerful Politburo and led the powerful political bloc that stood behind the policies of the Cultural Revolution, characterized by an ultra-leftist ideology and isolationism. The removal of the Gang of Four was conducted with surgical precision and with surprising ease. It was initiated by Hua Guo-feng, premier and vice-chairman of the Party; the respected Ye Jian-ying, also a Party vice-chairman; and elements of the People's Liberation Army. Hua soon became Party chairman. For the first time since the establishment of the People's Republic of China, the premiership and the party chairmanship were held by the same man.

Soon the Anti-Gang of Four Campaign began in earnest. It lasted over two years, from October 1976 until the beginning of 1979. Of the campaign's many objectives, three are of interest to us. First was the legitimization of the overthrow of the Four and the resulting new leadership. The strategy relied principally upon invoking the late chairman and wearing his spiritual mantle. Considering the tremendous prestige Mao enjoyed among the Chinese people and the role he played in New China, that strategy seemed the most rational. Expressions of dissatisfaction allegedly made by Mao about the Four were widely, though selectively, quoted.[4] Mao's alleged pronouncements and actions in support of the rapid political rise of Hua Guo-feng, especially since the death of Zhou En-lai, were publicized widely.[5] Overthrowing the Gang of Four was presented as an action that Mao had perceived as being eventually necessary but had not undertaken due to his declining health and untimely death. The overthrow was performed under the leadership of Hua, the man Mao allegedly chose as both Zhou En-lai's and his own successor.

Figure 1.   The Eve of the First Anniversary of the Death of Mao Ze-dong, Beijing, 1977.
Crowds and wreaths cover Tian An Men Square.
(Photograph by Author)

The second objective of the campaign was to effect a nationwide shake-up in all organizations at all levels. This was done to get rid of the "staunch supporters of the Gang of Four"; to put on notice those followers who were "misled" by the Four but were "willing to repent"; to restore gradually to positions of leadership those who fell victim to the Four's policies and actions; and to begin a massive reorganization in virtually every sphere of the country, including the administrative, political, economic, legal, educational and scientific sectors. Despite its magnitude and depth, this shake-up proceeded with minimal upheavals because of the leadership's deliberate effort to avoid repeating the Cultural Revolution's chaotic years and "to bring about great order across the land."[6]

Another major objective of the campaign was to expose and criticize the Gang of Four's deeds and ideology and to wipe out their "pernicious influence" on the people. Also, as expected, the campaign was to strengthen the ideological line of the new leadership and to instill it in the minds of the masses. To do so, a multitude of meetings were held at the grass-roots level, in the course of which ideologies and policies attributed to the Gang of Four were criticized. To bring the criticism closer to home, shortcomings within the work place and even the place of residence were linked to the Gang of Four. For instance, it was alleged that the major cause of the increased crime rate in urban areas had been the tolerance shown by the

Figure 2.   Euphoric Celebration of China's "New Liberation."
These festivities took place in Tian An Men Square, Beijing,
October 1, 1977—the first National Day following the downing
of the Gang of Four.
(Photograph by Author)

Gang of Four and its followers for criminal acts committed under the pretense of
political necessity. It was claimed that this tolerance had hampered urban authorities
in controlling crime. Moreover, the Chinese were required to study and discuss
the fifth volume of the *Selected Works of Mao Ze-dong,* published in the fall of
1977. It contained a careful selection of Mao's writings and speeches supporting
the current line, such as toning down class struggle and political campaigns and
stressing national economic development. The selection covered the post-Liberation
period from 1949 to 1957, but not beyond, when Mao's ideology took an ultra-
leftist turn.

Initial Post-Mao Economic Policies: The Four Modernizations Program

In addition to being ideologically, politically, and administratively anti-Gang of
Four, the campaign was also used as an important vehicle for redirecting the
country's life. Indeed, by criticizing the Gang of Four and contrasting its own views
with theirs, the new leadership was publicly indicating its position on a number
of questions and paving the way for new policies.

The First Session of the Fifth National People's Congress, held in Beijing beginning in late February 1978, outlined China's new economic policies. The Four

Figure 3.   Celebrating the Fifth National People's Congress, Beijing, 1978.
Portraits of Mao Ze-dong and Hua Guo-feng dominate the proceedings.
(Photograph by Author)

Modernizations Program was a blueprint for the rapid development of the national economy.[7] Its objectives were the "all-around modernization of agriculture, industry, national defense, and science and technology . . . so that our economy can take its place in the front ranks of the world" and to have "the output per unit of major agricultural products . . . reach or surpass advanced world levels and the output of major industrial products . . . approach, equal or outstrip that of the most developed capitalist countries."[8] These overly ambitious objectives were to be attained by the end of the century, a mere 23-year period. The view common among the leaders at the time was that if post-war Japan could modernize and build a powerful economy over two decades, China should be able to do the same. Their rationale was that, with the removal of the Gang of Four, a more orderly political and social climate and new and better policies, there was no reason why China should not be able to emulate Japan's economic rise using its superior socialist economic system.[9]

The Four Modernizations Program contained an initial ten-year (1976-1985) plan with exceedingly ambitious targets. The plan called for a rapid build-up of the economy on all fronts so as to bring the country to the take-off level by 1985.

In the agricultural sector, the report presented a number of targets to be reached by 1985: a 4 to 5 percent average annual growth rate in agricultural output between

1978 and 1985 (this rate had averaged 2.5–3.0 percent between 1957 and 1979); a 400 million ton goal for grain output (the 1978 figure had been 304.7 million tons); 85 percent mechanization of major agricultural processes (an obviously vague target); and the cultivation of one mu (equivalent to 0.4 acre) of stable high-yield farmland, irrespective of drought or flood, per capita of the rural population. Also, the report indicated, in a general way, how the government planned to increase agricultural output: by increasing non-grain output such as cash crops, fisheries, animal husbandry, and forestry; achieving a high rate of growth in marketable grain from key grain producing areas; reclaiming wastelands; developing non-agricultural economic activities such as rural industry; undertaking rural capital construction, including soil improvement and water control; encouraging more research in the agrosciences and more and better utilization of scientific production methods; and increasing production of farm machinery, fertilizer, and insecticide. The report ended by emphasizing the need to address many of the ideological, political and administrative problems that had been accumulating in the countryside since the beginning of the Cultural Revolution.[10]

The plan for the development of industry was no less ambitious. It called for high growth rates in light and heavy industries, and in transport and communications; for the "completion of an independent and fairly comprehensive industrial complex and economic system for the whole country," which was to be divided into six major economic regions; and for the rapid development of basic industries such as mining, and iron and steel.[11]

Among numerous projects of various sizes to be completed by 1985, there were 120 key ones to be undertaken by the central government. They included 10 iron and steel complexes, 9 non-ferrous metal complexes, 8 coal mines, 10 oil and gas fields, 30 power stations, 6 new trunk railroads, and 5 key harbors. Although new enterprises were to be established, the bulk of industrial growth was to come from existing enterprises. Indeed, the report called for special efforts to increase technical and managerial efficiency, particularly in the machine-building and defense industries and in capital construction, and for better coordination among small, medium and large-scale enterprises and their use of resources.[12]

The Four Modernizations Program was distinct from any attempt that had been made since 1964 at formulating a comprehensive developmental program. For the first time, the political environment was conducive to emphasizing national economic development. By February 1978, when the Fifth National People's Congress was held, the protracted battle for Mao's succession had been resolved. One major faction, the Gang of Four, had been eliminated. Two power centers at the top, those of Hua Guo-feng and Deng Xiao-ping, were coexisting. Despite basic differences simmering below the surface, there was a tacit understanding among the leaders that they should not rock the political boat and that the country should lose no time in embarking on an economic drive.

That the leadership saw the absolute necessity of launching a long-term economic drive is best understood in light of its belief that China had lost many valuable opportunities, but nonetheless possessed a great will and potential for national development. The political upheavals, campaigns and policies of the ten-year-long Cultural Revolution, and even of the Great Leap Forward, had extracted an economic toll. In the opinions of many Chinese leaders and economists, had such a situation lasted for another two or three years beyond 1976, a severe dislocation of the national economy would have occurred that would have compounded the political problems and threatened national security.[13] Also, contrary to socialist promises, the standard of living had not improved. In fact, in some regions, it had deteriorated.[14]

Apart from economic and social issues such as improving the living conditions of the people, the Chinese leaders considered politico-strategic issues paramount. They pointed out that world powers had successively intervened in China's internal affairs during the century preceding the establishment of the People's Republic largely because China lacked modern economic and technological bases, the foundation of national defense. Current Chinese leaders are sensitive to this question, and follow policies to prevent the country from slipping back into a situation that would make possible such intervention in the future. In his report at the First Session of the Fifth National People's Congress, Hua Guo-feng said: "We must race against time to strengthen ourselves economically and heighten our defense capabilities at top speed, for this is the only way to cope effectively with possible social-imperialist and imperialist aggression against us." So the Four Modernizations Program was "above all, an urgent political task."[15]

Setting the Ideological Scene

The word *xiandaihua,* or "modernization" in English, has probably never been used so often by so many people as it was in the first three years in post-Mao China. It was drilled into the minds of every Chinese, saturating the nation's propaganda channels: the media and political meetings. The campaign for modernization cleverly gave the word *xiandaihua* a mythical, almost magical meaning. When the Four Modernizations Program was announced in the winter of 1978, the scene had been set for its favorable, if not enthusiastic, reception by the people.

Usually, an important change in policy in China is preceded, or rather announced, by discussion in the state propaganda apparatus so as to justify it ideologically. This discussion usually follows a certain pattern: selectively using quotations from Marx, Engels, Lenin, Stalin or Mao, the media presents the ideological basis of the new policy as the correct one; at the same time, it attacks the opposing policy and its supporters. Barely perceptible in the beginning, the process builds to a crescendo, then gradually dies down when the opposition is presumed to have been silenced. In the case of the Four Modernizations Program, the Chinese leadership required economic policies that differed from those prevalent in the tumultuous Cultural Revolution. Therefore, they undertook to clarify the ideological bases of those new policies using the above-mentioned pattern soon after the removal of the Gang of Four.

One major attack on the Gang of Four's ideological stand was centered around the question of the relationship of politics and economics in a socialist state. The Gang was accused of distorting this relationship by giving a far more prominent role to politics than to economics. They were accused of misusing, for their own political aims, Mao's famous slogan: "Politics in command," greatly emphasizing class struggle and reducing all difference of opinion to it. The economy was thus greatly neglected. According to the propaganda, the correct view was that politics and economics should go hand in hand in a mutually supportive relationship. Politics should provide a propitious political and social environment for the country's speedy economic development, which in turn would strengthen the political system.[16]

Should an enterprise make a profit? Or does profit in a socialist economy reflect a capitalist mode of operation? Post-Mao Chinese media attacked the Gang of Four for having allegedly distorted the concept of profit in a socialist economy. Their argument was that, in a socialist economic system, profit was the source of accumulation and an accounting measure of efficiency, and was not exploitative.[17]

Another question concerned the principle of distribution of the economic pie. The new leadership considered income distribution policies in effect during the Cultural Revolution to have been too egalitarian, and thus labelled them ultra-leftist. It wanted to change that situation by following the Leninist tenet: "From each according to his ability, to each according to his work." In addition to conforming to Marxism and providing a just treatment of the question of workers' remuneration, this new policy was expected to create powerful incentives for better job performance, a crucial factor in the current drive for modernization.

The question of the role, nature, and degree of China's international economic activities within its national economy was reopened. Foreign interference in China's economy before 1949, and especially the dependency problems caused by Soviet economic aid in the 1950s, provided valuable historical lessons the Chinese leaders could not ignore. Since the Sino-Soviet Rift in 1960, the principle of self-reliance had been a major characteristic of the conduct of the Chinese economy. However, not surprisingly, there had been a wide range of views on what the practical meaning of this principle was and how it should be implemented.

In recent years, post-Mao leadership has reiterated its adherence to the principle of self-reliance, but at the same time it has vigorously criticized the Gang of Four's conservative and narrow interpretation of the principle. The Four were accused of pushing the Chinese economy into an almost autarchic state, thus shutting off the country from the benefits of foreign trade. The new leadership's position was that the principles of national independence and economic self-reliance would not be jeopardized with a sizeable expansion of foreign trade and a small dose of foreign financing, as long as China retained control and ensured that the foreign input fit in with economic development plans. Trade and debt were perceived as critical to expediting the transfer of foreign technology.

This seeming ideological shift was actually only one more phase of an ongoing tug of war between two different approaches to socialist construction: the one prevalent in post-Mao China and the one often referred to as "Maoist," which is best represented by the policies of the Great Leap Forward, the Communes Movement and the Cultural Revolution—all launched by Mao himself. What characterizes this latest shift is Mao's absence from the political scene.

Reforms

To create an atmosphere conducive to rapid economic development, the post-Mao leadership introduced major reforms in the political, economic, educational, social, legal and cultural spheres after 1977. Many of these reforms are still in the process of being implemented and are considered but one stage in a long overhaul of China.

Once more, the policy of "Let a Hundred Flowers Blossom, Let a Hundred Schools of Thought Contend" was revived.[18] Its purpose was to encourage freer expression in political, scientific, artistic, cultural, and other circles. Later, Deng Xiao-ping and his supporters advocated that actions should follow an objective analysis of the question at hand ("Seek Truth from Facts") rather than conforming to whatever Mao Ze-dong had said or had done ("The Two Whateverisms"). Unlike the decade-long Cultural Revolution, when the media was used to propagate the "correct" lines and views and to attack anything that did not conform, the post-1977 media was less dogmatic, often reporting the varied, but acceptable, views expressed in the course of debating questions of national importance.[19]

Stifled by the Cultural Revolution, the arts were revived beginning in 1978. Many famous classical operas were performed after being banned for a decade. Film production, albeit of uneven quality, increased rapidly, was more attuned to popular taste, and treated wider and more daring themes, such as love and questions of daily life. The political messages in musical performances were toned down and at times eliminated, giving way to a greater concern for entertaining the public and using a variety of styles, including Western.

Priority was given to the modernization of Science and Technology, which was considered the key to the Four Modernizations. Following many debates within the Chinese Communist Party, the government and scientific circles in 1977 and 1978, important decisions were made and actions taken. In 1977, the Chinese Academy of Sciences was revitalized, and the Chinese Academy of Social Sciences was founded. A new pro-scientific atmosphere was fostered across the country, a noticeable change from the situation prevalent during the Cultural Revolution. A National Science Conference was held in Beijing in March–April 1978, the first of its kind. From it emerged the Draft Outline Program for the National Development of Science and Technology (1978-85), which contained the overall plan for national scientific activity for those seven years.

In the education sector, a new policy was formulated and a new system set up. It was designed to meet the perceived needs of the country's modernization in terms of popular education and adequate professional training. Unlike the educational policy of the Cultural Revolution, this new policy emphasized education by expanding curricula and raising standards. In the fall of 1977, university admission reverted back to a highly competitive national examination system so as to select the academically best qualified students, with much less regard to their social and political backgrounds than had been the practice during the Cultural Revolution. Also, an atmosphere more conducive to serious studies was fostered in schools and universities, in contrast to the high political militancy encouraged during the Cultural Revolution, when political factions used students to destroy their rivals.

Although substantially more resources were allocated to education, they were still inadequate as measured against the national need.[20] Educational facilities had to be rebuilt, upgraded or enlarged. The standard of living and the academic level of faculty members had to be raised. Long neglected scholarly and academic exchanges with the outside world had to be reestablished and expanded. Taking the risk of creating a new elite, the Chinese government decided to concentrate some of its scarce resources on the training of young professionals in designated key educational institutions. To allow the proper implementation of these measures, the educational system underwent a thorough overhaul, in terms of both its administrative structure and its personnel, from the education minister down to local staff.

In the decade-long Cultural Revolution, and for brief periods before that, China's legal system had been in the hands of the party and the police. It was characterized by the enforcement of "socially approved norms and values inculcated by political socialization and enforced by extrajudicial apparatuses consisting of administrative agencies and social organizations."[21] Such a legal system resulted in much abuse, due to a high level of subjectivity and lack of impartial legal procedures. In their attempts to remedy the problem of abuse and to set the judicial scene for a modern country and economy, the Chinese authorities are currently designing a system based on a wide variety of laws and administered by a judicial hierarchy: the police, the procuracy, and the courts. The first set of laws, seven in number, was adopted by the National People's Congress in 1979, and others have followed since then.

Concurrently with the introduction of reform in their respective professional fields, intellectuals—artists, writers, educators, legal workers, scientists—have received very different treatment by the authorities. During the Cultural Revolution, with a few exceptions, they had been the object of policies that often disrupted not only their professional but also their personal lives. Labelled the "ninth stinking category," intellectuals were seen as still upholding a bourgeois ideology incompatible with a socialist society.[22] They were also resented for their mental work and were forcibly "reeducated" through manual labor.[23]

To remedy the anti-intellectual stand of the Cultural Revolution, and to gain the crucial participation of intellectuals and professionals in the country's economic drive, post-Mao leadership took a series of measures favorable to them. The political dossiers of thousands of people, many of whom were intellectuals accused of being anti-socialist, were reopened for review. The great majority of those reviewed were rehabilitated politically. Their social, professional and financial status was thus restored. Many were compensated for the damage they had suffered. An effort was made to have them work in areas for which they had been trained, and to correct the past arbitrariness of their job assignments. Henceforth, their contributions to society would be measured in terms of achievement in their respective professional areas rather than in their participation in political discussions or manual labor. They were also encouraged to become more involved in the management of their work organizations and in defining their work.[24]

The Need for Economic Readjustment

Criticism of the Four Modernizations Program surfaced soon after it was announced in February 1978 and possibly even before then. The earliest and most notable criticism of which we are aware was that voiced by Hu Qiao-mu, president of the prestigious Chinese Academy of Social Sciences. He submitted a critical report to the State Council in July 1978, which was not published until October 1978.[25] Hu had two major messages for the Chinese leadership. The first was that China's socialist economic system would not automatically bring about the successful and rapid economic development of the country. He felt there was no guarantee that basic objective economic laws would be observed, nor that correct policies would be implemented. He pointed out that there had been a sorry tendency in China to ignore basic economic laws and rely more on political and administrative measures to run the economy. He also thought China should shift its priority of developing heavy industry to developing agriculture and light industry.

His second message was that a basic problem inhered in the management of the national economy, and that reforms should be introduced to reduce bureaucratic barriers and stimulate the initiative of producers. He advocated setting up industrial trusts; using a contract system to conduct economic transactions between enterprises, rather than the rigid planning system; granting the banks a more active role in the decision-making and control of enterprise investments; and establishing an economic and commercial legal framework to regulate relations between the State and enterprises and among enterprises.

Why were the economic problems not seen when the Four Modernizations Program was drafted a few months before? The answer put forward through official propaganda channels was twofold: when the Four Modernizations Program was submitted in early 1978, the leadership did not have a clear picture of the post-Mao economic situation.[26] As a result, the Four Modernizations Program was inadequately prepared. Also, the pace of economic growth was too fast for the economy to absorb. Indeed, in 1978, the Gross Industrial and Agricultural Output Value went up 12.3 percent; total foreign trade, 30.3 percent; the national budget (both revenues and expenditures), about 30 percent; and capital construction, 31.3 percent (see tables 1 and 2).[27]

Table 1. Key Economic and Foreign Trade Indicators, 1978–80

	1978 ACTUAL Total	1978 ACTUAL % Change	1978 PLAN % Change	1979 ACTUAL Total	1979 ACTUAL % Change	1979 PLAN % Change	1980 ACTUAL Total	1980 ACTUAL % Change	1980 PLAN % Change
1. Total Gross Industrial and Agricultural Output value (Billion Yuan, 1970 Prices)	569.0	12.3	10.4	617.5	8.5	7.0	661.9	7.2	4.0
2. Gross Value of Industrial Output (Billion Yuan, 1970 Prices)	423.1	13.5	11.9	459.1	8.5	7.9	499.2	8.7	5.6
—Heavy Industry	242.4			261.1	7.7	7.6(1)	264.8	1.4	5.4(2)
—Light Industry	180.7			198.0	9.6	8.3(1)	234.4	18.4	6.8(2)
3. Gross Value of Agricultural Output (Billion Yuan, 1970 Prices)	145.9	8.9	6.2	158.4	8.6	4.4	162.7	7.7	-0.6
4. Percentage of State-Owned Enterprises Running a Loss	24.0			23.7			23.3		
5. Retail Price Index (%)				5.8			6.0		
6. Total Foreign Trade (FOB/CIF)	35.50	30.3		45.5	28.0	24.0(1)	56.3	23.6	13.6(3)
—Exports (FOB)	16.76	20.0		21.2	26.6	14.7(1)	27.2	28.3	
—Imports (CIF)	18.74	41.1		24.3	29.6	32.4(1)	29.1	19.2	
—Trade Balance (Exp.) Less Imp.	-1.98			-3.1			-1.9		

(1) Yu-Qiu-Li, "Report on the Draft of the 1979 National Economic Plan," in Main Documents of the Second Session of the Fifth National People's Congress of the People's Republic of China, Beijing 1979.

(2) "China's 1978-79 Economic Results and 1980-81 Plan Targets," The China Business Review, Jan.-Feb. 1981.

(3) Yao Yi-Lio, "Report on the Arrangements for the National Economic Plans for 1980 and 1981," Beijing Review, September 22, 1980.

Sources: State Statistical Bureau, Communiqué on the Fulfilment of China's 1978 National Economic Plan," Beijing Review, July 6, 1979.
——; "Communiqué on the Fulfilment of China's 1979 National Economic Plan," Beijing Review, May 12 and 19, 1980.
——; "Communiqué on the Fulfilment of China's 1980 National Economic Plan," Xinhua News Agency, April 29, 1981.

Table 2. State Financial Data, 1978–80

	1978		1979		1980	
	Total	% Change	Total	% Change	Total	% Change
1. Annual State Budget (Billion Yuan)						
A. Revenues (Domestic Funds)	112.111	28.2	106.80	-4.74	104.22	-2.4
Revenues (Incl. Foreign Loans)			110.33	-1.59	108.52	-1.6
B. Expenditures (Domestic Funds)	111.093	31.7	120.30	8.29	113.97	-5.3
Expenditures (Incl. Foreign Loans)			127.39	14.67	121.27	-4.8
C. Balance (Domestic Funds)	1.018		-13.50		-9.75	
Balance (Incl. Foreign Loans)			-17.06		-12.75	
2. Capital Construction (Billion Yuan)						
A. Total Investment of which	47.9	31.3	50.0	4.4	53.9	7.8
National Budget	39.5	34.0	39.5	0.0	28.1	-28.9
Provinces, Localities & Enterprises	8.4	20.0	10.5	25.0	25.8	145.7
B. Investments by Type of Activity (Percent of Total)						
1. Nonproduction	17.4		27.0	55.2	33.7	24.8
2. Production	82.6		73.0	-11.6	66.3	-9.2

Sources: Zhou Jing-fu, "Report on the Final State Accounts for 1978 and the Draft State Budget for 1979," in *Main Documents of the Second Session of the Fifth National People's Congress of the People's Republic of China,* Beijing 1979.

Wang Bin-gian, "Report on Financial Work," *Beijing Review,* September 29, 1980.

———, "Report on the Final State Accounts for 1980 and the Implementation of the Financial Estimates for 1981," *Xinhua News Agency,* December 15, 1981.

State Statistical Bureau, Communiqué on the Fulfilment of China's 1978 national Economic Plan," *Beijing Review,* July 6, 1979.

———, "Communiqué on the Fulfilment of China's 1979 National Economic Plan," *Beijing Review,* May 12 and 19, 1980.

———, "Communiqué on the Fulfilment of China's 1980 National Economic Plan," *Xinhua News Agency,* April 29, 1981.

Figure 4.   A Street Demonstration, Shanghai, 1979.
Demonstrators demanded that "educated youth" return from the
countryside and that young unemployed be given jobs.
(Photograph by Author)

The true sources of the economic problems were seen, however, as being the poor management of the economy and the imbalanced economic development of the past two decades.[28] There were a number of important imbalances between various economic sectors: agriculture and industry, light and heavy industry, energy and other industries, investment and consumption, and capital construction and rural industrial production. Also, opponents of Hua Guo-feng saw the announcement of the ambitious Four Modernizations Program as Hua's political move to herald his new era as the new chairman of the Communist Party and as government premier.

Despite the fact that since the Great Leap Forward the stated policy has been that agriculture should be the foundation of the economy, not enough resources have been allocated to it. According to the June 1981 World Bank report on the Chinese economy, the gross agricultural output grew by 2.5 to 3.0 percent between 1957 and 1979, yet agricultural output per worker dropped 12 percent between 1957 and 1977.[29] Per capita food consumption reached the 1930s level only in 1978.[30] Within the agricultural sector, despite repeated official pronouncements urging balanced agricultural production, there had been too much emphasis on grain production at the expense of industrial crops, animal husbandry, forestry, and fisheries.

In addition, too much emphasis had been placed on developing heavy industry. In the 1950s, following the Soviet model, China had given high priority to the development of heavy industry to set up a national industrial base. Although such a policy must have been justified then, its continuous implementation for close to three decades became counterproductive. The rate of industrialization was slowed because many scarce resources were tied up in long-term projects instead of in quick turnover investments in light industry. Eventually, heavy industry itself suffered from the ensuing slow generation of funds. The people's standard of living also decreased because of the economy's high rate of investment in heavy industry and the lack of consumer products from light industry. Lack of both resources and attention hindered the development of a light industry that could compete on the international market.

The energy industry had not kept pace with the country's needs due to poor planning and sizeable waste in industrial use.[31] This greatly hindered industrial production. It was estimated in 1978 that, due to shortage of electric power, about 20 percent of China's production capacity was idle. Many key plants were producing well below capacity due to lack of materials. The country's infrastructure was not properly developed to handle its high economic growth. For instance, in segments of major trunk railway lines, only 50 to 70 percent of the freight could be handled. Extractive industries could not keep up with demand.

Another major imbalance was between investment and consumption. The rate of investment had been very high in order to sustain a rapid development of heavy industry, resulting in strains on the economy. The people's standard of living was adversely affected because disproportionately higher funds were allocated to capital construction for industry and defense at the expense of such sectors as housing, education, culture, research and health care.

A major source of problems was the management of the economy. In the early 1950s, China adopted the Soviet economic management system, i.e., a highly centralized planned economy. Central to the economic life of the country was the plan (one-year, five-year, or ten-year). Production quotas and directives were transmitted through the plan to all industrial and commercial enterprises and to agricultural communes and farms. Each economic entity came under the jurisdiction of at least one vertically structured administrative organization, whether regional (e.g., central, provincial or local), sectorial (e.g., machine-building or mining industries), or functional (e.g., marketing or financial).[32]

This type of structure naturally tended to create an overconcentration of power. Very little leeway was left to enterprises and local authorities for production, marketing and supply decision-making. Enterprises received all their funds for both investment and operations as appropriations from the State according to plan and in turn remitted their profits, if any, and retained only inadequate funds for equipment repair and maintenance.[33] If registering a profit, the enterprise might obtain a bonus proportional to its wage bill, principally for distribution among its workers. Production output was delivered to enterprises or government departments according to plan. The enterprise had little choice in the selection of personnel, which were assigned by the responsible labor department. With such an overconcentration of power at the upper levels, the enterprise found itself lacking both the capability and incentive to manage itself efficiently.

The activities of each of the economic subsystems, such as the iron and steel, machine-building and chemical industries, were determined by the plan, which supposedly regulated the national economy. Yet because of the highly vertical structure of these subsystems, and their insulation from market pressures due to their monopolistic positions, poor and irrational results were sometimes observed. For instance, in 1979, 20 million tons of steel, the equivalent of about 60 percent of that year's production, were overstocked because of low quality, inappropriate specifications, hoarding, or simply an inability or unwillingness to find takers. Yet, China imported special steels of about the same quantity, some of which could have been produced domestically with little effort.[34] In addition, the vertical structure and lack of market pressures had created the "small yet complete" and "big yet complete" syndrome. Regardless of their size, ministries and enterprises tried to be as self-sufficient as possible in their respective operations. Of course, a sizeable amount of waste resulted.

More often than not, decisions were based more on administrative and political than on economic criteria. This fact led to many economically irrational decisions. An unnecessarily high proportion of projects or enterprises were not economically feasible.[35] The pricing system and structure, based principally on those of the 1950s, had changed little. The great overlap between central and local government departments in jurisdiction over the enterprises made the implementation of any system of economic responsibility and accountability complicated, if at all possible.[36]

Readjustment: Phase I

Two major and interrelated events took place at the Third Session of the Eleventh Central Committee of the Chinese Communist Party, held in December 1978 in Beijing. The first was a decision made by the Chinese authorities to put the economy on a path different from that of the Four Modernizations Program. The communiqué issued at that session stated that

> there are still quite a few problems in the national economy, some major imbalances have not been completely changed and some disorder in production, construction, circulation and distribution has not been fully eliminated. A series of problems left hanging for years with regard to the people's livelihood in town and country must be appropriately solved. We must make concentrated efforts within the limits of our capabilities to carry out capital construction actively and steadily, and not rush things, wasting manpower and materials.[37]

The communiqué stated the need to decentralize some of the economic decision-making power; to pay attention to economic laws; to prevent interference by the Party, government and enterprises in one another's functions; and to adopt a system of reward and punishment. It also pointed to two major shifts in the national economic policy: (1) giving much more importance to the development of agriculture, and (2) improving the people's standard of living through measures that would increase the national consumption rate. The communiqué itself was not explicit as to the new direction the economy might take or how such a change would be accomplished. Clearly, more realistic economic plans and programs had to be worked out to replace the overly ambitious Four Modernizations Program.

The other major event that took place at the Third Session was the appointment of Chen Yun to the position of vice-chairman of the Communist Party, which automatically made him a member of its Politburo Standing Committee. Chen had been known for his mastery in running the national economy and for having twice reinvigorated it after major crises—first, immediately after the Chinese Communist Party came to power in 1949 following a long civil war, and second, after the infamous Great Leap Forward. Because of his opposition to the Great Leap Forward, he had lost all his official posts. His return to the apex of political power meant that the economy was experiencing serious problems and strict measures would be taken to remedy them. Chen was clearly the architect of the economic policy shift announced at the Third Session. In July 1979, he was made vice-premier and chairman of the newly established, yet powerful, State Financial and Economic Commission, so he could direct the implementation of the new policy.

The new policy was presented officially at the Second Plenary Session of the Fifth National People's Congress in June 1979 in Beijing. Known as "Readjust, Reform, Consolidate and Improve," the policy had the objectives of readjusting the imbalances in the economy, reforming the national economic management system, restructuring and consolidating economic sectors and enterprises, and improving the economy as a whole.

First of all, agriculture, and not heavy industry, was to be put at the top of the nation's list of economic priorities. To encourage a high growth rate in the agricultural sector, the Chinese government took actions on three separate levels: restoring and strengthening communes' rights, reforming the management of the agricultural sector, and raising procurement prices. Those measures were announced and implemented as early as the fall of 1978. Communes, production brigades and production teams would have their economic rights, e.g., ownership of their assets and decision-making power, strengthened and guaranteed by the State. Those rights had often been interfered with by higher level authorities, which had at times appropriated their manpower, products or funds without proper compensation. A remuneration system intended to reflect better the work output of the peasants was to be implemented. At the same time, the use of private plots was to be protected and encouraged. The team would be kept as the basic accounting unit in the three-level organization structure of the commune and would have its economic power strengthened. A more democratic system for selecting commune leaders at all levels would be introduced. To stimulate agriculture and improve the peasants' income, state purchase prices of agricultural products were raised by about 20 percent, and by 50 percent for above-quota production. More funds were also allocated to the agricultural sector in the State budget.[38]

Soon the Chinese government seemed to be pushing for drastic reforms in the agriculture sector. Government and administrative functions were removed from the communes and placed at the county level, limiting the former to being basically economic institutions. Following experimentation in selective rural areas, the responsibility system was introduced gradually in the countryside. In that system a peasant family or an individual contracts with the commune to produce a certain amount of agricultural output, a portion of which is to be sold to the State at set procurement prices. Any excess output is retained by the family or individual for consumption or sale at the burgeoning free markets. The producer has free rein as to the management of the production. Combined with the recent hikes in agriculture prices, the responsibility system should be one of the most powerful incentives established in China since 1949.

To adjust the imbalance between light and heavy industries, the overall growth of heavy industry would be slowed, in terms of both production and investment, while light industry would receive an increased share of investment funds and higher priority in the allocation of energy and materials. To help light industry develop more rapidly and become more competitive on the international market, China was to import technologically advanced capital goods and begin to tap foreign managerial, technical and marketing expertise, through joint ventures, compensation trade, buy-back and other similar arrangements with foreign corporations.

Cutbacks in heavy industry were effected selectively. Sectors such as the machine-building industry that were considered to be receiving an unduly high proportion of resources had their growth rate cut and were encouraged to produce more needed consumer goods. Sectors such as the steel industry that were poorly attuned to the demands of the economy were under pressure to gear their production to meet the requirements of the new economic policy. Other sectors such as mining energy, building materials and infrastructure (transportation and communication), which constituted serious bottlenecks in the rapid development of the economy, received a sizeable injection of investment. Sources for such funds were domestic as well as foreign, including both loans and direct investments.[39]

Measures were taken to increase the national consumption rate and improve the standard of living. These moves included a reduction in the proportion of funds allocated to capital construction; budgetary increase in investments for social projects such as housing, cultural, educational and health care; an increase in personal income in both the agricultural and industrial sectors; and a push for production of more consumer goods.[40] To expand production, more emphasis would be put on enlarging, streamlining and using the available production capacity of existing enterprises, rather than building new plants.[41] This shift in policy was designed to save a substantial amount of investment, contribute to the running of a more efficient economy, and cut back on heavy industrial construction.

To remedy the overconcentration of power at the top, decision-making was decentralized in many areas. Provincial and local governments saw their economic power augmented not only administratively but also financially, through a higher retention rate of funds that normally went to the central government. At the same time, managers were accorded more authority in running their enterprises within the confines of the national plan (cf. chapter 2).

Concurrent with the decentralization of the economic and managerial decision-making authority, and to keep policy and strategic decisions in the hands of the central government, new commissions were established under the State Council. These commissions played the crucial roles of integrating and coordinating national economic affairs and controlling the proper implementation of the new policy.[42]

To encourage the use of economic rather than administrative criteria in the conduct of economic affairs, a large number of governmental departments were organized into business corporations. Measures were undertaken to reorganize and restructure many of China's industries. The overlapping of jurisdictions among government departments was reduced. Also, vertical as well as horizontal mergers of enterprises were effected for more efficient operations. Unprofitable enterprises were pressured to shut down, to switch to alternate businesses, or to merge with more profitable ones. Instead of trying to be self-sufficient, more and more enterprises resorted to subcontracting. This trend contributed to the reduction of waste created by the "small yet complete" and "big yet complete" syndrome and was facilitated by the introduction of market elements into the economy.

To reform the economic management system and effect the proper implementation of the above-mentioned measures, the Chinese authorities moved to introduce what the noted economist Xue Mu-qiao called a "market regulation" of the economy in addition to the "plan regulation."[43] Considering the ideological connotations, this move was rather bold. Market elements in a fundamentally socialist economy could not be well developed nor strong. Yet their marginal roles could alleviate many of the problems that the central plan could not, or had itself caused. For example, to remedy the imperfection of the supply-demand mechanism in a centrally planned economy, communes and enterprises were allowed to sell their surplus output directly on the open market. They were permitted some flexibility in setting prices. It was hoped that they would thus become more efficient in their operations since they would be facing open competition. To improve the employment situation, and to provide more consumer services, the establishment of small collective and privately owned enterprises was facilitated in sectors such as catering, local transportation, and even the construction industry.

Readjustment: Phase II

The policy of readjustment began to be implemented even before its official announcement. Yet it was not until well into the second half of 1979 that the readjusted plans, which had first been introduced in selected industries and enterprises, began to be enforced generally.

Given the performance of the economy for the years 1979, 1980 and most of 1981, the readjustment policy met with much success. Yet there were signs of serious problems lying ahead. Following is a brief discussion of the main outcomes of the readjustment policy.

The emphasis on developing the agricultural sector resulted in a substantial increase of output for both years, 1979 and 1980. Output responded to increases of the state procurement prices announced during the fall of 1978 and to the push for peasants to market privately both their above-quota output and that of their private plots. The additional autonomy, which the communes enjoyed at all levels, often allowed more rational production decisions, and thus a higher output. The result was a jump in output in 1979, which registered an annual growth rate of 8.6 percent, almost double the 4.4 percent planned rate. In 1980, output grew at 2.7 percent despite adverse natural conditions. A decline of 0.6 percent had been expected (see table 1).

The shift in economic policy to boost light industry was translated into a number of measures that allowed a high growth rate for this sector. Some of those measures included a small though effective increase in capital construction funds, an increase in the State allocation of energy and materials, and a significant increase in the import of technology and materials. The result was an impressive growth rate of that sector: 9.6 percent and 18.4 percent in 1979 and 1980, respectively. Both rates were above those planned, particularly that of 1980, which had been set at 6.8 percent (see table 1). In the first six months of 1981, light industrial output grew but at a lower rate compared to 1980, and it was expected to register an 8 percent annual growth rate.[44] However, for the first time since the Great Leap Forward, the value of light industrial output rose to over 50 percent of all industrial output, and thus topped that of heavy industry.

In 1979, the heavy industry growth rate (7.7 percent) was closer to the revised planned rate (7.6 percent). Yet that sector's performance in 1980 uncovered serious problems. Although output of heavy industry was 6 percent higher in the first six months of 1980 than for the corresponding period in 1979, its annual growth rate was only 1.4 percent for all of 1980. This statistic indicated a serious decline in production during the second half (see table 1). The output for 1981 was forecast to register a growth of 1 percent at best, but it actually fell.[45] This poor performance was explained by the deliberate policy of reducing the overall growth of heavy industry, restructuring it, and updating much of its outdated technology. Heavy industry was clearly going through a painful, though necessary, transition period.

The growth rate of capital construction—mainly capital investment in industry and infrastructure—was much more difficult to bring under control. At the time of the announcement of the readjustment program in 1979, it was stated that funds allocated for capital construction in the State budget would stay the same as in the previous year. Indeed, this was true, and the State spent 39.5 billion yuan for capital construction. However, the total national capital construction continued growing due to a number of factors including: 1) entrenched group interests (for example, circles in heavy industry were dragging their feet in reducing their investment); 2) the momentum capital construction had acquired in China's economy; and 3) the often inefficient means of selecting and implementing projects. The non-

Figure 5.   Common Means of Transportation in Medium-size and Small Cities
and in the Country.
(Photograph by Author)

State share of capital construction grew from 8.4 billion yuan in 1978 to 10.5 in 1979 and 25.8 in 1980 (see table 2). This growth, of course, continued to put pressure on national resources regardless of the sources of funds.

Although the Chinese economy performed rather well in 1979 and 1980, it began to show signs of strain in 1980 because of problems that had either existed prior to 1977 or had been created by the readjustment policy itself. In February 1981, Premier Zhao Zi-yang said that "the most serious problems in China's economic readjustment this year consist mainly of cutting back capital construction and expenditures, and striking a basic financial balance. The economy must be stabilized to avoid potential danger."[46]

Since 1978, when the statistic became available, about 25 percent of the State-owned enterprises have experienced operational losses in post-Mao China. These losses have been caused by: 1) structural factors, such as pricing policy and the management of the economy; and 2) a highly inefficient enterprise management. In many industrial sectors, production technologies were far from efficient, in terms of both energy consumption and productivity.

Despite the reforms implemented in the management of the economy, and partially because of them, problems in the circulation and distribution of commodities persisted. On the one hand, enterprises and other economic organizations helped alleviate the imbalance that existed between supply and demand through substantial production increases. Enterprises enjoyed their newly acquired autonomy and were spurred on by the new policy of "regulating" the economy through both the market and the plan mechanisms. On the other hand, a few problems arose, mainly due to the inability or the inexperience of the Chinese planners and decision-makers in handling some of the unexpected effects of "market regulation." For instance, commercial enterprises, which until then had enjoyed a virtual monopoly over commodities circulation, found themselves unable to command their supplies as before. The bidding on the "open market" for much needed products contributed to the inflationary pressures the economy has experienced since 1978. Finally, because of great inefficiency in the "market," producers of raw materials were reluctant to supply the State with their output. Communes producing industrial crops preferred either to set up or to enlarge their own enterprises to process their output. Consequently, they reduced the supply of those materials to the urban market, thereby causing underutilization of production capacity. The overall effect was to lower economic efficiency and reduce the quality of products in the effected industries.[47]

In an attempt to shift China's economic developmental strategy further from what the West calls its "Maoist" mode, the strategy of "Yangzhang Biduan, Baohu Jingzheng, Zujin Lianhe" ("Develop Merits and Avoid Shortcomings, Protect Competition, [and] Promote Cooperation") was made public in mid-1980.[48] This strategy meant that China should use its comparative advantage to develop its economy. For example, enterprises that best produced high quality, profitable goods should be encouraged to expand their production while less efficient enterprises should decline or cease to exist. Similarly in agriculture, a region should produce those crops for which it was best suited, rather than crops that could be bought from other parts of the country on favorable terms. For example, Hainan Island should produce rubber, a crop more suited to its climate, rather than grain. To do so, free commodity flow should be possible. Regions should not take measures to protect less efficient production, as had been the case, and interregional competition ought to be allowed for the sake of economic efficiency.

This strategy directly addressed the sensitive issue of the developmental gap between various regions in China by suggesting that cooperation should be promoted between more developed areas, such as Shanghai and Tianjin, and less developed areas, such as Anhui and Qinhai Provinces. The gap should not be allowed to widen. Such cooperation had taken place before but was not viewed as successful enough by the Chinese leadership. The reason for past failure, it was suggested, had been both political and ideological. The basis for the new cooperation should be principally economic: joint ventures, compensation trade and contractual arrangements should be set up between enterprises of different regions for their mutual benefit.

The major implication of this strategy was that there was now in Beijing a stronger belief in developing an integrated, regionally interdependent economy.

Figure 6.   Low-Tech Snow Clearance Organized by the
Neighborhood Committee, Wuhan, 1978.
(Photograph by Author)

This belief in commodity flows among regions contrasts with the "Maoist" economic strategy of semi-self-reliant regional development, which had previously been in effect. The tendency now was to look at the economy as a whole rather than as the sum of its regional parts.

Inflation was another major outcome of the economic policies instituted in post-Mao China. Before 1976 China prided itself on having an inflation-free economy. But in 1979 and 1980, China made public the increases registered in its Retail Price Index, which were 5.8 and 6.0 percent, respectively, for the two years.[49] This price increase resulted from a combination of actions taken by the authorities, including:

a new income policy, which raised income substantially in both the rural and urban areas without linking it with similar increases in productivity;

the policy of increasing the financial power of local governments and enterprises, which, with the expansion of the market elements in the economy, tended to force up prices of commodities that were in short supply;

budget deficits, the result of continuous pressures on expenditures, due to the authorities' inability to cut capital construction, increases in non-production project investments (e.g., housing, education, and science), a higher wage bill, and higher State purchase prices for agricultural produce (coupled with State subsidies for staples). This situation was aggravated by a reduction of the central government's portion of revenues derived from local governments and enterprises (see table 2).

A number of measures were adopted to control the rising inflation rate. In late 1980, the State Council issued its regulations on price control. To counteract some of the confusion that might have resulted from the introduction of "market regulation," a clarification was provided as to which types of commodities were subject to pricing by the State and which to market fluctuations. Teams were also formed in various parts of the country to investigate improper pricing activities by enterprises.[50] To offset partially the 29.16 billion yuan combined budget deficits for 1979 and 1980, the State Council issued treasury bonds in 1981. Bonds purchase quotas were allocated to local governments, enterprises and the army. In the first part of 1981, close to 5 billion yuan were thus brought under the central government's control. Finally, the 1981 capital construction budget was reduced by 44.3 percent from the previous year, to 30 billion yuan.

China's economic development has been adversely affected by an inadequate energy supply and infrastructure. Even if addressed with vigor, these two bottlenecks will exist for a number of years, since their remedy requires sizeable amounts of resources and time. Coal and oil output have not changed significantly since 1979 and 1980 despite increasing demand. Substantial increases cannot realistically be expected in the very short term. To tap its vast coal reserves, China has increased investment to replace outdated mining equipment and to open up new coal mines, using an increasing proportion of imported technology. The production of the promising offshore oil is expected to start soon on a large scale with the injection of national and foreign capital. The speed with which these investments will become productive, and the results of the current efforts to use energy more rationally, will play a crucial role in the rate of economic development.[51]

Despite the fact that China has done well in developing its infrastructure in the last three decades, there are still weaknesses in areas such as transportation and telecommunications. For instance, China's harbors are far from capable of handling the substantial increase of traffic due principally to the growth of foreign trade, which more than doubled between 1977 and 1980. In February 1981, "a

Figure 7.   Normal Sunday Shopping on Nanjing Road, Shanghai, 1979.
(Photograph by Author)

daily average of 353 ships had to wait in ports," and, even when all frozen harbors thawed, the average was still as high as 276 for the month of May 1981.[52] The transportation bottleneck has been so serious that it has come to the attention of Chinese leaders at the highest level.[53] Sizeable investments have been allocated to expand and modernize the transportation and telecommunication systems, some of which have come from foreign sources, e.g., Japan and the World Bank.

The policy of reducing the growth of heavy industry compared to agriculture and light industry has recently come under open criticism, in terms of both its cost to society and its incorrect implementation. A good proportion of the capital assets of heavy industry has been sitting idle. Hundreds of thousands of workers have been laid off, and yet they have been collecting their pay from the State. Questions have also arisen as to the correctness of reducing capital investments in heavy industry, as a matter of principle. This sector provides greatly needed equipment for mining, power and light industries, as well as for the development of the national infrastructure, all of which have been top priorities. In the second half of 1981, statements made by Chinese leaders and actions taken by economic organizations indicated a modification in policy towards heavy industry so as to encourage more balance and coordination between light and heavy industry.[54]

Postscript

The first half of this decade has seen a steady, rapid and widespread growth of the reform trends begun in the late seventies. Probably the foremost factor for the consolidation of the direction in which China has embarked is Deng Xiao-ping's success at spreading his power across the country's political chessboard, leaving no sphere—political, legal, economic, educational, artistic—untouched. He and his closest supporters succeeded in initiating the long process of technocratization of the Party and the higher echelons of the government by smoothly replacing the old revolutionary cadre with younger, more educated leaders committed to modernization and reforms. The fact that Deng's restructuring of the leadership was undertaken without the upheavals, pains and costs of "class struggles" of Mao's China not only demonstrates that he has been in full control, but also that he intends to introduce a more moderate style of political management strikingly different from that of his predecessors.

A cornerstone of Deng's modernization of the political system has been the parallel introduction of a more democratic style of decision making within the Party—Chen Yun's publicly questioning aspects of Deng's policies in his widely-reported speech at the Party's National Conference held in September 1985 had no precedents in socialist China—and of a body of laws and regulations, though still embryonic, with the intention to regulate social and economic life in China and to avoid past experiences of the rule by one man and the excesses of the personality cult.

The Chinese economy, which performed well from 1977 to 1979, began to show signs of strain in the second part of 1980 and was facing real difficulties by 1981. A period of austerity combined with a more serious implementation of the Readjustment policies was necessary to combat inflation, budget and balance of payment deficits, and the side effects of the restructuring of major industrial sectors. These efforts put China's economy in the enviable position of experiencing about a 10 percent annual growth rate for the four-year period ending in 1985.

Economic reforms have been a resounding success in the agriculture sector, which has basically adopted a tenant farming system, removing the stifling control of the State and developing a commodities market in the countryside where 80 percent of the population live. The removal of price and crops production controls, the burgeoning of small-scale industrial enterprises and of the service industry in the countryside and the unquestionable sizeable improvement of the peasants' standard of living attest to the success of the agricultural reforms.

Reforms in industry, though successful, have not been as impressive as those in agriculture. Entrenched interests, political constraints, systemic inertia and the complex characteristics of the structure of the industrial sector did not allow the widespread implementation of efficient market mechanisms, price reform and enterprise management reforms (see chapter 2). The Chinese leadership introduced with vigor its bold "Open Door" policy to attract foreign investments to boost transfers of technology, capital and management know-how to China. The policy seems to be fulfilling its objectives though falling short of the leadership's high expectations and not without elaborate efforts made by foreign and domestic parties to ensure the success of their ventures.

Whether judged against her own past experience or the reforms in other centrally-planned economies, China's economic performance and reforms of the seven-year period ending in 1985 are truly impressive. They have propelled the country in a direction which would be extremely costly to reverse. To be able to pursue the long and difficult course the country has embarked on, China must enjoy a long period of political stability and be in a position to tackle some of the more difficult and sensitive reforms such as that of the pricing system.

2

Early Post-Mao Reforms of State-owned Industrial Enterprises

Basically, the task of a socialist industrial enterprise is to carry out at the grass-root level the mission of a consolidated dictatorship of the proletariat. Lenin pointed out that "Socialism is the abolition of classes." To fulfil the historical mission of Socialism, socialist enterprises must take class struggle as the key link, adhere to the Party's basic line, stick to a socialist direction in enterprises, struggle against capitalist and all exploiting classes; [they] must organize the whole staff in studying Marxism, Leninism and Mao Ze-dong thought.

Industrial Enterprise Management,
The Economics Department, Hebei University, 1977.

The basic task of a socialist industrial enterprise is to produce more, faster, better and cheaper material goods (or to provide labor services), and to create even more profit. That is, with the least possible input of human, material and financial resources, and through its own activities, it outputs for the society the most possible industrial products (or industrial services), profits and technical personnel, and it creates the proper conditions for the society to expand reproduction and to raise the standard of living of the people.

Management of Chinese Socialist Industrial Enterprise,
People's University Press, 1980.

We are going to implement major reforms of our economic management system and of our enterprise management system. Five years from now, if you take a look at China, you will not recognize it.

A Senior Professor of Management in Shanghai, 1979.

Introduction

After the establishment of the People's Republic of China in October 1949, it took seven years to socialize the national economy. Upon winning the civil war, the Communist Party immediately extended its control over key sectors, such as banking and steel, and implemented land reform. Other economic sectors such as commerce were brought gradually under its control. At the same time, its influence over still privately held businesses grew through economic, organizational and political measures. In 1956, in the course of China's First Five-Year Plan, the Chinese authorities completed the "socialist transformation" of its economy. Economic activities were undertaken in organizations whose assets, or means of production, were held by the collective (principally in agriculture, handicrafts and light industry) or by the State (principally in heavy industry, extractive industry, commerce, and banking). Private undertakings still existed but were insignificant in terms of the total amount of generated business, limited in scope by strict regulations and relegated to marginal activities.[1] In the 20-year period (1956–1976) that followed, this socialist transformation evolved in two important ways. First, in 1958, during the controversial Great Leap Forward, the People's Communes were established, subsuming all economic and governmental organizations in the countryside below the county level. In non-agricultural sectors, the State took an increasingly important position in the national economy at the expense of the collective sector (outside the commune system) and of the private sector, which to all intents and purposes disappeared during the Cultural Revolution. For instance, in 1973, State-owned industrial enterprises possessed 97 percent of industrial assets, produced 86 percent of industrial output value, and employed 63 percent of industrial workers.[2]

The result of the socialist transformation was a highly centralized, planned economic system, at the core of which were the plans: long-term plans, five-year plans and yearly plans. Hundreds of thousands of people administered the system at all levels and phases: setting national economic policy, drawing up the plan, and implementing it in its most detailed form. They were part of a mammoth pyramid at the apex of which sat the top leadership of the Communist Party, who set national economic policy. Immediately below them were the executive branch of the government, headed by the State Council with all its ministries, commissions and other offices and bureaus. The State Council was required to articulate the economic policy into operational policies and plans and to ensure that the policies and plans were implemented. All the centralized ministries and other State Council institutions that dealt directly with the economic life of the country were organized in ways that reflected products, services, functional and regional divisions. Except the People's Communes, local governments set up their own administrations along these divisions to govern the economic activities that fell within their jurisdiction.[3] The result was an administrative body that was ponderous, cumbersome, pervasive, yet necessary for a centrally planned and run economy.

At the base of this pyramid were the numerous enterprises producing goods and services according to the plan. At the turn of the 1980s, China had close to 400,000 State-owned enterprises in industry, communication and transportation, including 80,000 factories.[4] Each one of these enterprises belonged administratively to at least one of the offices in the pyramid, at a level determined by: 1) the strategic and economic importance of the enterprise, 2) its size, 3) the relative bargaining power of each governmental level, and 4) the history of its development. Collective enterprises, ideologically less glamorous, technologically less advanced and economically less important than their State-owned counterparts, belonged administratively to local governments, usually at lower levels. In 1980 under the commune system, China had 1.43 million communes and brigade-run factories (some of which would barely qualify as workshops) with a labor force of 30.5 million workers, equivalent to 10 percent of the rural labor force, and an annual income of 61.4 billion yuan or 34 percent of the total income of the commune system.[5]

In the view of the Chinese leadership, the People's Republic of China had a good record in building a national industrial base, despite poor performances during such periods as the Great Leap Forward and the Cultural Revolution. The leadership also felt that such an industrial base was an excellent foundation for their modernization and economic development drive. Yet they became increasingly aware during 1977 and 1978 that, unless major changes were introduced in national economic policies and in the system of enterprise management, the country would not be in the position to undertake that drive successfully. In the previous chapter, the shifts in economic policies and the reform of the economic system resulting from the Eleventh Party Congress in 1978 were introduced briefly. As further background to subsequent chapters dealing with management practices, this chapter outlines the reforms of the management system of State-owned enterprises introduced since late 1978.

Before we look at the reforms, a brief definition of what constitutes an industrial enterprise in China is helpful. The majority of industrial enterprises are one-factory organizations, which are considered independent production, legal and accounting units that possess some decision-making power, principally on matters directly related to the management of their operations. The factory may have a number of workshops and the staff organization necessary for its proper management. There are some multi-factory enterprises, which combine a number of factories into one business entity in a variety of ways. There may be a number of feeder factories linked to the main assembly plant, e.g., in the automobile sector; they may be vertically or horizontally integrated, e.g., in the metallurgy, oil and textile sectors; or they may all be specialized in the same type of manufacturing processes or products, such as casting, power generation or industrial meters and instruments. Often such enterprises are named *gongsi*, i.e., "company" or "corporation," particularly when member factories could have been or were enterprises in their own right. Other corporations, also called *gongsi*, control a number of enterprises belonging to the same industrial sector. These corporations are purely administrative, not engaging in producing goods or services nor owning production assets. Basically, they are an arm of the government, dealing in economic matters—a type of administrative holding corporation. Since the introduction of the reforms, more multi-factory enterprises, corporations and conglomerates involved in the production of goods and services have been formed. Also, new types of enterprises have been created, notably consulting companies and joint ventures between Chinese as well as between Chinese and foreign enterprises.

All State-owned enterprises, regardless of type, are required to produce according to their share of the national plan. This requirement substantially limits their authority over what and how much to produce, over input sourcing and product marketing, and over pricing. Also, decisions on most matters not directly related to daily operations lie within the jurisdiction of governmental offices and administrative corporations. Included are those decisions concerned with long-term strategy and policy of the firm, operational policies, the selection of management personnel above a certain level, research and development, and so on. Thus, many strategy and policy functions performed by staff in a capitalist corporation's headquarters typically are absent from its Chinese counterpart, having been moved upward within the economic system. The smaller and less prestigious the enterprise or corporation, the less influence it is likely to have on these policy decisions. At the risk of oversimplifying, in terms of its internal management and the scope of its power and responsibilities within the Chinese economy, a one-factory enterprise in China may be compared to a plant of a large corporation in a capitalist country, and a large multi-factory corporation, to its tightly controlled division.

Reforms of Chinese Industrial Enterprise Management (1978–81): An Overview

Clearly, were it not for its economic role in the production of goods and services, an enterprise would not exist as such. It is an organization that, in post-Industrial Revolution societies, constitutes one of the basic building blocks of the national economy. By its very existence, the enterprise also plays a political role, protecting or furthering its interests through political channels, among others. The interests can be those of the enterprise as a whole; its various constituents, e.g. owners, managers and workers; or third parties, e.g. governments, unions and the society at large. In addition, the very fact that it provides work for its members, and indirectly for others in the society, means that it plays a social role as well.

Among the enterprise's several roles, the economic and the politico-ideological roles have had a fascinating dialectical relation in the People's Republic of China, which is summarized by Mao's slogan: "Grasp Revolution, Promote Production." The importance of the economic role of Chinese enterprises in national economic development, first in non-agricultural sectors and then in the economy as a whole, has been documented already.[6] The political role of preserving and furthering the enterprise's interests within the national economy has also been present in China, as it has in all economies. However, of special interest are those aspects of the enterprise's political role that result from the fact that China is a socialist country.

The Chinese leadership has adopted its version of Marxism as a guiding ideology in its governance of the country's affairs, including the national economy. Its socialist world view includes the historical materialist explanation of society, incorporating the desire to steer the nation away from capitalism and into an inevitable socialism. One power base used to attain such an objective is economic. Also, as a materialist political philosophy, Marxism considers the economic base a long-term determinant of the superstructure, i.e., the political, cultural, social, and educational systems. Thus, to establish and consolidate its own power within a socialist society, the Chinese Communist Party had to control the means of production in order to control the economic base. The enterprises' political role then becomes conscious, deliberate, firmly based in theory, and indeed crucial to the success of the newly established order.

These and other theoretical bases to the enterprise's political role in a socialist society are not seen in Marxist terms as impeding production or economic life in general. As the slogan: "Grasp Revolution, Promote Production" leads one to believe, it is through making socialist revolution, i.e., establishing and exercising proletariat dictatorship and setting up a socialized economy, that the nation's economy is expected to develop rapidly. Consequently, a dialectical relationship will exist between the economy and politics in society in general, and between the economic and political roles of the enterprise in particular. Theoretically, this relationship should be mutually supportive.

The purpose of this short discussion is to make the following two points, which help illuminate the political basis to the reforms of enterprise management undertaken in China since 1978. The first is that, notwithstanding the number of shifts in the Chinese Communist Party's governance of the national economy in the last 30 years, its guiding ideology has remained well within the range of Marxist ideology. The current reform of enterprise management should likewise be seen as Marxist, since it preserves the basic foundations of the Chinese socialist economy, although the leadership intends to manage them differently.

The second point is that, at times, politics has in fact hindered the economy. Theoretically, the dialectical relation between politic and economics allows for the "Grasp Revolution" mandate to have some minor and temporary negative effects on the "Promote Production" notion. But in reality the Chinese experience has shown that the effects have been more severe than expected or desired. The Chinese leadership now believes that politics has hindered, if not endangered, the national economy twice in the last two decades—during the Great Leap Forward and the Cultural Revolution. Whether, in the eyes of this leadership, these two instances were cases of simple overdoses of the appropriate (political) medicine, or the administration of an entirely wrong medicine, is a question that should be the subject of further study. Suffice it to say that in 1978, the Chinese leadership perceived the need to reform enterprise management as the result, among other things, of one of those unfortunate practical outcomes of the relation between politics and economies. Yet, this outcome does not invalidate the dialectical relation between politics and economies. Rather, the leadership has simply concluded that the economic side of the equation should take on greater importance and politics should be more supportive of economic activity. It is quite possible that this relation may revert in the future to a mode in which politics again hinders the economy.

Figure 8.   "Walking on Two Legs," Hu County, Henan Province, 1978. Rural industry to support agricultural production.
(Photograph by Author)

In its first major practical step to reform enterprise management, the Chinese leadership decided to modify the structure of upper management. During the earlier part of the Cultural Revolution, factory directors were replaced with revolutionary committees as the executive arm of the enterprise. These revolutionary committees were comprised of representatives from the People's Liberation Army, the Party and enterprise staff. When the upheavals of the Cultural Revolution began to subside, the army's representation was removed gradually. Among the many purposes of setting up these committees were the introduction of collective leadership, the institution of a wider representation in upper management, and restoration of the enterprise to normal operations after bitter and divisive struggles.[7] As before, the revolutionary committee operated under the Party committee, whose functions included representing the Party at the lower organizational levels and exercising control over ideology, policy, and workers' welfare as well as over the enterprise's major decisions, such as production plan formulation, incentive system and so on.

In 1978, the Chinese leadership decided to re-institute the "system of responsibility of factory director under the leadership of the Party Committee" (*dangwei lingdaoxia de changzhang fuzizhi*). Thus, each enterprise was required to replace its revolutionary committee with a director and deputy-directors. The rationale was that, while revolutionary committees might have been useful before, they were becoming increasingly inadequate for managing enterprises at a time when China was poised for a new economic development drive. The principal complaint heard about the revolutionary committees concerned their inability to make decisions efficiently and run the daily affairs of the enterprises. It was felt that with the re-institution of the position of factory director, lines of responsibility would be clearly demarcated and decisions would be made quickly, thereby providing a better and faster response to the needs of the enterprise.

There had been strong criticism of this system during the Cultural Revolution on the grounds that it 1) concentrated too much power in the hands of the directors; 2) it was undemocratic; and 3) it placed too much emphasis on production and too little on political and ideological questions. The Chinese leadership argued, however, that all these problems stemmed from poor implementation of the system rather than from its inadequacy per se. To remedy these problems, and with the benefits of past experiences, the directors would operate under stronger Party committees, would be held responsible for their performance, and would face an enterprise with increasing democratic participation through the Workers Union and Workers Congress.[8] It was not clear what measures had been taken to strengthen the supervisory role of the Party committee over the director or the workers participation in the management of the enterprise.

The re-institution of the factory director position was a prelude to deeper reforms of enterprise management. The central leadership in Beijing, with the strong backing of Deng Xiao-ping, approved a pilot project to assess the reform of enterprise management. In October 1978, six enterprises in Sichuan province were selected for the experiment, conducted under the leadership of Zhao Zi-yang, a protégé of Deng, who was then the Party secretary of that province.[9] By January 1979, their number was expanded to 100. Of these, 84 were locally run industrial enterprises; the others were in transportation and telecommunication. The enterprises were selected so as to represent various sectors and trades and various administrative levels to which enterprises were subordinated (Lin Ling, 1980). To be selected, an enterprise had to demonstrate, among other things: (1) a strong and capable leadership group; (2) the reorganization and consolidation of its management; (3) an ability to produce goods for which inputs were secure and a market was readily available (Lin Ling, 1980); and (4) a growth capacity (Kasper, 1982).

Sichuan provincial authorities issued a set of new regulations to govern the operations of enterprises taking part in this experiment. The purposes of these regulations were threefold: 1) to regulate a totally new type of venture for which there was little precedent in the People's Republic of China, 2) to unify as much as possible the conditions for this experiment within each of the participating enterprises; and 3) to provide the participating enterprises with an environment favorable to improving and expanding their businesses.

These regulations allowed participating enterprises, unlike others in China, to: 1) produce beyond their State-imposed production plans, 2) sell goods not purchased by State commercial organizations directly on the market, 3) retain a percentage of their profits, 4) retain as an incentive to develop new technologies and processes all the profits acquired through these means for two years, 5) retain for worker bonuses a sum based on their fulfillment of State targets, 6) make promotion decisions about middle-level management, 7) pay a low interest on working capital exceeding the preset funds quota and high interest on capital required because of overstocking, rather than no interest at all, 8) retain a portion of their foreign exchange earnings to import new technology, equipment and material, and 9) decide how to distribute bonuses.

In April 1979, less than four months after the expansion of the Sichuan experiment to 100 enterprises, the State Economic Commission held a conference in Beijing to launch another experiment in enterprise management. Eight factories were selected to take part in that experiment, three in Shanghai, three in Beijing, and two in Tianjin. The purpose of this new experiment was to have these enterprises, which were among the most successful and best managed in China, act "as pioneers and explorers, and build up experience in [the] consolidation [of the enterprise] and in the proper use of the authority transferred down [to the enterprise], then expand [the experiment]" and "make a summary of a set of enterprise management methods which will be appropriate to the needs of a China-type modernization."[10]

A number of areas were singled out for special attention on the part of the enterprises in this experiment. Six of these areas were:

1. To keep the functions of the Party and of the enterprise directorship separate under the newly established "system of responsibility of the factory director under the leadership of the Party Committee."
2. To implement a strict quality control system and to develop brand names, new products and new product lines.
3. To strengthen business accounting and improve management results.
4. To provide, according to a set plan, management training for the cadres and professional training for the staff.
5. To improve the wage and incentive system so as to relate it to the performance of the staff and the enterprise.
6. To improve work conditions, including safety and democratic participation of the staff in the management of the enterprise through the Worker Congress.

It is interesting to note that in addition to being considered well-managed and successful, the eight enterprises were located in three of the largest and most important industrial centers, close to major centers of economic decision-making. They were all large enterprises, prestigious and influential, with direct communication lines to central authorities. As in the Sichuan experiment, enterprises were allegedly given expanded management autonomy, and the experiment was carried out under the direction of the highest local Party organization, the municipal Party committee in each city. The eight enterprises were required to make regular reports on the conduct of this experiment, and more particularly on the problems they were encountering due to the inadequacies of the economic management and enterprise management systems. In July 1979, the State Council decided to extend this experiment to 4000 enterprises throughout China and to allow the participation of other-than-industrial sectors such as construction, commerce, transportation and material supply.

The third major step in this national experiment in reforming the enterprise management system was to establish a group of enterprises that would operate experimentally on a profit and loss basis. Enterprises taking part in this new experiment were made responsible for their business operations and the ensuing profits or losses; in return, they were allowed to retain their after-tax profits. In early 1980, five enterprises that had been part of the Sichuan experiment were directed to be "responsible for profits and losses" (*zifu yunki*).[11] By late August 1980, five enterprises outside Sichuan were selected to be part of the new experiment. Three of the non-Sichuan organizations were in Beijing and the other two in Shanghai. Being responsible for profits and losses did not mean that these enterprises were not required to operate according to the State plan. They were still obliged to fulfil their production plan. However, they had a freer hand in their operations than other enterprises. In a way, they became profit centers, financially responsible for their own operations within a socialist economy, clearly a delicate and ambiguous state of affairs in China.[12]

More specifically, these *zifu yunkui* enterprises were supposed to be accorded a new set of rights and obligations, in addition to the still applicable rights of self-management given to enterprises taking part in the previous experiments. The most important of these new rights were: 1) to pay taxes and fees rather than remitting all profits to the State;[13] 2) to buy and sell capital goods, though under state regulations; and 3) if additional funds were needed to apply to the People's Bank of China for loans by proving the economic feasibility of the project and to pay interest on the loans if granted.

Undertaking this new *zifu yunkui* experiment was a bold move on the part of the Chinese leadership in view of its politico-ideological implications. They stressed that enterprises taking part in the experiment still had to operate within the plan, that they remained State-owned, and that they had to obey a set of strict regulations. But to many more orthodox Marxists, such enterprises contained elements of capitalism. At least, they were seen as being placed in a situation that might encourage capitalistic tendencies. Such enterprises might operate in ways incompatible with, and contradictory to, the idea that production assets should be owned by all of the people and controlled by the State.[14] Yet, according to some Chinese economists, the *zifu yunkui* system was the ultimate objective of the reform of the enterprise management system. Lin Ling stated that

> The objective of enlarging the right of an enterprise to self-management is to liberate it from the fetters of the current system, and to make it truly a relatively independent commodity producer. But this objective cannot be attained in one stroke. There must be a multi-stage process which we envisage to be roughly as follows: first, [we must] undertake the profit retention [system], and correspondingly enlarge the power of the enterprise in [production] plan formulation, product sales, expansion of production, and other such areas; after that, [we must] realize [the system of] independent accounting, substitution of tax [payment] for profit [retention], [and] responsibility for profits and losses.[15]

By the fall of 1980, three separate and parallel systems of managing State-owned enterprises prevailed in China. The first was the "enterprise fund system," also referred to as the "little reform" (*xiaogai*) system. This system consisted of providing enterprises that have fulfilled all State targets with a fund for yearly bonuses equal to a preset, yet not nationally uniform, percentage of the enterprise's total payroll. In terms of operations, such enterprises did not enjoy any of the autonomy afforded to enterprises taking part in the reform experiments. For instance, they were bound by production, supply, personnel, sales, financial and other decisions made by their superior administrative organizations. In principle, they were not allowed to expand their production beyond the State plan nor sell their goods on the open market. The "enterprise fund system" was instituted across China during the three years after the death of Mao Ze-dong in 1976, and provided some limited incentives for better enterprise performance—thus the name of *xiaogai* or "little reform." This type of enterprise constituted the basically non-reformed enterprise management system in China.

The second system was that of "expand the enterprise right for self-management," also known as the "middle reform" (*zhonggai*). This system was, as noted above, at the core of the Sichuan experiment and the eight enterprises experiment. The third system was that of "responsibility for profits and losses," also known as the "big reform" (*dagai*). In terms of the use of the enterprise's accumulated funds, whether retained earnings as in the case of the *zhonggai* or after-tax profits as in the case of the *dagai,* these two systems are similar. In both cases, the State required that the accumulated funds be allocated to three major funds within the enterprise: 1) bonus funds, to be distributed according to performance; 2) welfare funds, to be used to build or improve housing and recreation facilities, day care centers, canteens and so on; and 3) production funds, to be disbursed for projects directly related to production but outside the normal operating budget, such as expanding production, introducing new products or new product lines, innovating, and improving production technologies and equipment.[16]

As long as it conformed to the basic guidelines set by the State regarding the proportion allocated among the three funds and the types of expenditures allowed within each, the enterprise was free to decide how to spend its after-tax profits or retained earnings. Accumulated funds are allocated about equally between the three funds, usually slightly favoring the production funds. Mechanisms were set whereby the enterprise management, its workers and its Party committee all had a say in the expenditures of each of the three funds. But in reality, the management exercised greater control over the production funds, while the workers, through the Workers Congress and the Workers Union, and the Party committee were more interested in the use of the other two.

By April 1981, based on official data, the situation seemed to be as follows:

1. In Sichuan, 417 industrial enterprises had expanded their right of self-management, 407 of which were in the *zhonggai* mode, and the other 10 in the *dagai*. These 417 enterprises produced 70 percent of the output value, 80 percent of the profits, and 90 percent of the profit remittances to the State of all provincial (local) industrial enterprises. Of the 417,238 commercial enterprises had developed self-management, 139 in the *zhonggai* mode and 99 in the *dagai*. In addition to industrial and commercial enterprises, a few in other economic sectors (e.g., banking, transportation, industrial materials supply and marketing) had also developed self-management.[17]

2. On the national level, including Sichuan Province but excluding Tibet where these reforms had not been introduced, there were 6,000 State-owned industrial enterprises enjoying an expanded right of self-management.

Although they constituted less than 16 percent of the total number of State-owned industrial enterprises in 1980, they produced 60 percent of the total output value and 70 percent of the total profits of the State industrial sector.[18]

3. All State-owned enterprises not included in the *zhonggai* or the *dagai* programs were of the *xiaogai* type.

The management and operations of State-owned industrial enterprises were affected not only by these reforms, but also by macroeconomic measures taken principally under the rubric of "Consolidate and Improve," part of the "Eight-Character Policy," i.e., "Readjust, Reform, Consolidate and Improve." It is important here to mention briefly their key elements to understand their impact on enterprise management reform.

One of the main "consolidation" measures taken by the Chinese authorities was to deal with the large number of enterprises experiencing operating losses. According to China's State Statistical Bureau, between 23 and 24 percent of State-owned enterprises sustained losses in 1978, 1979, and 1980, and 27.1 percent in 1981. One should question the validity as well as the meaning of such figures, and the concept of loss, for several reasons. Very low depreciation rates, and little if any cost of capital have been traditionally used in the accounting system of Chinese State-owned enterprises. In many instances, blame for losses may be put on the outdated and irrational (in terms of representing the degree of scarcity and value of commodities) pricing system set by the State Council. Even so, it is clear that a high proportion of enterprises were unprofitable principally due to poor management both on the macro level (e.g., the pricing system, research and development policy, poor plan formulation and implementation, an inadequate marketing system, etc.) and the micro level (e.g., internal management). The Chinese leadership wanted to cut down enterprise losses, particularly those caused by inefficient micro management. It took drastic measures, closing some of the unprofitable enterprises. The operations of others were suspended, pending further action, or merged with other enterprises. Many were ordered to retool their plants so as to switch production from goods in excess supply or of poor quality to goods in demand.

On an industrial sector level, structural inefficiencies had built up over the years. For example, in January 1980, the then Vice-Premier Bo Yi-bo reported that the automobile industry in China included 130 factories, which produced 160,000 cars a year. These numbers, he said, ranked China as first in the world in number of car factories, but 22nd for production of cars.[19] Due to underdeveloped market mechanisms in a centrally planned socialist economy, and the ideological biases the Communist Party had retained from the period of guerrilla warfare, most enterprises preferred to operate as independently and self-reliantly as possible. They built in-house facilities for auxiliary production and services that would have been less costly to subcontract, especially for the smaller enterprises. At the very time such an approach was encouraged, enterprise representatives would quote with pride the Chinese idiom: "Maque sui xiao, wuzang ju quan" ("the sparrow may be small, but it has all the vital organs," that is: small yet complete). Interregional and intersectorial economic relations among enterprises were burdened with all sorts of bureaucratic and economic factors, plus many conflicts of interest. This tendency toward enterprise autocracy has been criticized by the Chinese as the "independent kingdom" mentality. All these and other factors prompted the Chinese leadership to take measures to restructure and consolidate many of China's economic sectors and enterprises. Some of the principal measures are listed below:

1. By the first quarter of 1981, 19,336 enterprises (or 5.13 percent of all State-owned enterprises in China) were merged or reorganized into 1,983 specialized companies or general plants, 236 of which have been taking part in the experiments related to enterprise management reform. Some of these new companies specialized in providing a certain process or service such as casting and forging or thermal treatment, to other enterprises in large industrial centers. Others were the result of merging enterprises along both vertical and horizontal lines. For example, in the textile industry existing enterprises were amalgamated into companies spanning the production of raw materials (such as cotton or wool), spinning, printing and dyeing, and marketing up to the final consumer. In addition, the reorganization of entire industries, such as the automobile industry, eliminated enterprises entirely, merged others and created entirely new companies. This reorganization was concentrated mainly in Beijing, Shanghai and Tianjin, where 30 percent of all municipal enterprises have been affected, and began to extend to other industrial and commercial centers.

2. Three thousand four hundred domestic joint ventures, compensation trade enterprises, and contractual arrangements were set up across regions, economic sectors and between enterprises with differing types of asset ownership (State-owned, collective and individual). These new types of economic associations were established to secure the supply of capital goods, parts, semi-finished products and raw materials from the countryside, to market manufactured products, and to undertake research and development projects.

3. To improve the quality of enterprise management, younger and better educated cadres were promoted to management positions, and training for executive managers and other professionals was widely provided (see chapter 4).[20]

Preliminary Summary Assessment of the Reforms of Enterprise Management

Scanning Chinese professional journals relating to experiments in enterprise management reform, one notices a pattern in the evolution of the themes and tones of the articles that parallels the evolution of the experiments themselves. Prior to the official start of an experiment, when the decision to undertake it had already been made unofficially among a core of top leaders, articles appeared emphasizing the need for various measures to remedy particular deficiencies in China's economic and management systems. Basically they were position articles, the purposes of which were, among others, to establish a need for the measures, to test the waters, and to inform the public in which direction the country would be heading. More professional articles followed, dealing on a general level with how to implement such measures. The public was then exposed to preliminary reports on how an enterprise taking part in the experiment showed instant improvement in its management, operations and, hence, economic performance. After providing rather impressive statistics to illustrate these results, an author might mention a series of rules and regulations or current practices prevalent in the economic system in China that have been shown in the first few weeks or months of the experiment to impede its proper implementation. The author naturally requests that the authorities take appropriate action. Subsequent articles add a section dealing with implementation problems lying within the enterprises' jurisdiction, and urge the enterprises to remedy them. A few months after the anniversary of the start of each experiment, the public is given summaries of its good results, citing somewhat more credible statistics, followed by a review of the problems encountered during implementation. The causes of these problems may be traced to the authorities, factors within the enterprise, the current economic system, or to the design of the experiment.

From the high and constant praise the experiments received in the propaganda channels, it is clear that the Chinese authorities were convinced that reforming enterprise management was long overdue. It is also clear that, according to official data, the results were favorable, and that the authorities were committed to implementing long-term managerial reforms at the enterprise level. The Chinese leadership seemed determined to deal realistically with the myriad of problems that appeared. In this section, a brief review of the results and problems is presented, followed by a few analytical thoughts on these experiments.

The management and employees of the 6,000 reformed enterprises seem to have recognized that they were offered powerful incentives to run efficient and profitable operations. Individual and group bonuses, welfare funds, and retained earnings earmarked for production were all linked directly to profits. To take advantage of new opportunities, many enterprises adopted new modes of operations. For example, market research and promotion were undertaken to an extent unheard of before. With their newly found financial power, enterprises allocated funds for innovation and technical improvement, often reaping sizeable benefits within a very short period of time by taking advantage of market inefficiencies and the pent up demand for products.

Many enterprises instituted more efficient planning and control systems, streamlined daily operations, and reduced traditionally high inventories. They improved their internal organizations by creating marketing and after-sales service groups and strengthening the accounting and finance departments. Many such enter-

Figure 9.　Beijing Wool Blankets Factory, 1978.
The board with ''red flags'' shows the workshops that have fulfilled state monthly and quarterly quotas.
(Photograph by Author)

Figure 10.　Beijing Wool Blankets Factory, 1978.
Keeping track of the fulfillment of population control objectives at the factory level.
(Photograph by Author)

Figure 11.   Beijing Wool Blankets Factory, 1978.
Propaganda team putting up the news from the Fifth National
People's Congress.
(Photograph by Author)

Figure 12.   Unusually Clean Workshop, Beijing Wool Blankets Factory, 1978.
(Photograph by Author)

prises preferred to work with other organizations on a contractual basis. Such contracts may spell out rewards and penalties relating to the performance of the task in question. With their new freedom to produce and sell goods on the market beyond their State production quota, many enterprises were in the position to alleviate some of the problems created by the economic slowdown China encountered in 1980. For instance, in the case of Sichuan, 30 percent of participating enterprises received a State production quota well below their production capacity, and hence were compelled to produce for the market to maintain profitability.

The overall improved performance of enterprises taking part in the experiments was indicated by the aggregate statistics published in China. According to official statistics, in 1979, 84 of the 100 industrial enterprises taking part in the Sichuan experiment increased output value by 14.9 percent, total profits by 33.5 percent and the profits remitted to the State by 24.2 percent over 1978. Their performance was higher than the average performance of all State-owned enterprises in the province. In 1980, the total output value of the 417 enterprises in the Sichuan experiment rose by 9.66 percent and their total profits by 7.43 percent over 1979. However, due to profit-sharing formulas that often favored the enterprises, and to the effects of the readjustments policy and other serious economic problems that China faced in 1980, the remitted profits decreased by 3.7 percent. But an even larger decrease, 30.3 percent, was registered by enterprises not taking part in the experiment.[21]

Of the 6,000 enterprises that took part in the national experiment, 5,777 local industrial enterprises (this number excludes enterprises taking part in the *dagai* experiment and enterprises controlled directly by the central authorities) raised their 1980 output value by 6.8 percent, their profits by 11.8 percent and their hand-in profits by 7.4 percent over the previous year.[22] Shanghai's 1,284 industrial enterprises that were part of the experiment likewise performed well above average. In 1980 as compared to 1979, their total output value increased by 7.4 percent (against a 5.3 percent increase for the whole of Shanghai's industrial sector); their profits, by 6.9 percent (against Shanghai's 3.7 percent); and their remitted profits, by 4.1 percent. Beijing's 110 enterprises that took part in the experiment in the second half of 1979 increased their output by 12.7 percent over 1978; their profits, by 9.9 percent; and their remitted profits, by 6.5 percent.[23]

As expected in such experiments, many problems were encountered. First, the distribution of profits between the State, local governments and the enterprises was a serious issue. Often, to encourage an enterprise to participate in the experiment, formulas for distribution of the profits were agreed upon that were clearly unduly generous to the enterprise. Also, as an incentive to overfulfil profit quotas, formulas included a progressive rate for retained profits beyond a preset base. Typically, hard bargaining took place, with the enterprises trying to set the profit base even lower than the planned profit quota. For example, the average enterprise in Jinan and Qingdao municipalities in Shangdong Province had a profit quota 17 percent and 14 percent, respectively, above the preset profit base, and it was

Figure 13.   1976 List of Advanced Workers in a Textile Factory, Beijing, 1978.
(Photograph by Author)

estimated that it would retain 60.42 percent and 51.40 percent of excess profits, respectively. Clearly, these proportions seemed too high to many Chinese observers.[24]

Another problem was the distribution of bonuses. This question has been hotly debated due to its ideological and political implications. Enterprises were urged not to keep the "egalitarian" system of bonuses, which divided the bonus funds more or less equally among the workers with little consideration for performance. Many felt pressure to move away from the "egalitarian" system and increase workers' purchasing power, but they lacked experience in implementing economically feasible and fair bonus systems. As a result they gave their workers unduly high bonuses with the funds they had begun to accumulate. In an effort to control this situation, the State Council issued directives and guidelines that limited, among other things, the total yearly bonuses to the equivalent of two months' wages. Even so, excesses in this area continued to be reported. For example, again in Jinan and Qingdao, the number of workers whose wages and bonus system was based on the piece rate method (in practice a more advantageous method to the worker, given the adoption of low standard rates) increased 2.3 times and 4 times, respectively, in the second half of 1981 compared to the same period in the previous year. In the first nine months of 1981, in Qingdao, the average income (wages

Figure 14.   Textile Factory, Beijing, 1978.
(Photograph by Author)

and bonuses) of workers taking part in the piece rate system in both state- and collectively-owned enterprises was 63.81 percent higher than the average income of the total worker population of that municipality. There was a serious gap between the income received by workers who were on the piece rate system and by those who were not. The average income of the first group (or 50.32 percent of the total work force in Qingdao) was 4.63 times that of the second group (or 49.68 percent of the work force), creating a politically serious situation.[25]

With their newly found autonomy in production and marketing, enterprises took actions that were economically rational in terms of their own interests but raised serious questions elsewhere. For example, in the face of basically fixed prices of inputs and outputs, enterprises naturally increased production of the more profitable goods and reduced the production of the less profitable, despite the product mix of their State production quotas.[26] This policy created supply problems for the latter type of goods. To increase their profits and retained earnings, enterprises overfulfilled their production quotas of goods that the State was supposed to market and pressured State commercial enterprises to purchase their excess outputs, when they were unable or unwilling to market them directly. This activity created serious cash flow and overstocking problems. In many instances, enterprises would themselves sell this type of market restricted product on the open market. They could command a premium because of the availability of the product or the convenience to the buyer of avoiding the red tape and delays imposed by the State commercial enterprises. In addition, instances of serious reduction in product quality or in workers' safety were observed in enterprises seeking quick profits.

The implementation of the experiment often led to confusion. For instance, no clear delineation of jurisdiction was possible among the various commissions (economic, financial, materials supply, marketing, planning) and other organizations with a direct say in the conduct of these experiments. This confusion created conflict and waste among all involved, inducing many of the reformed enterprises to voice their complaints. Despite the number of measures and regulations issued by the State Council, many enterprises and government organizations were not always clear as to what was permitted and what was not. For instance, during interviews conducted in late summer of 1980, I received contradictory information as to the right of an enterprise to sell a portion of its capital goods. Some enterprise managers were under the impression that they were eligible for incentives for innovations and new products they introduced. Yet they did not actually qualify. In addition, basic business mistakes were committed. Enterprises entered into ventures using their own funds, without adequate market research prior to investment commitments. Supply of inputs was not secured or buyers were hard to find.[27] At times these new ventures were not efficient and drained inputs away from those already established. These events further complicated the consolidation and restructuring of the industrial sectors the government was undertaking.[28]

There was a growing discontent among enterprises, whether taking part in the experiments or not, about the inequalities that resulted from these experiments. The Chinese coined the expression *kule bujun* ("uneven hardship and happiness") in reference to the phenomenon. Often the size of enterprises' rewards, e.g. retained profits, was unrelated to the quality of its management. Factors that contributed to this inequality were, among others, 1) the extent to which an enterprise faced a favorable price schedule as fixed by the State; 2) the condition of the enterprise's production technology (and, hence, the level of its productivity); 3) the enterprise's bargaining power in extracting better profit sharing terms; and 4) the system of rewards which often favored enterprises that were poorly managed (because they presented larger margins for improvement than those of the well managed enterprises, rewards being often a function of marginal improvement).

Enterprises that were not selected for these experiments felt that, for reasons over which they had no control, they could not profit from the new set of incentives. Average income of workers in these non-reformed enterprises did not keep up with their counterparts' in those subject to reform, and thus the reform was perceived as placing the welfare of their workers at a relative disadvantage.

Let us examine two fundamental questions that have been raised regarding the experiments themselves. The first concerns the design of the experiments, more specifically the method of selecting the enterprises. Not only were the best and largest enterprises chosen for the experiment,[29] but in Shanghai, while participating enterprises increased their output by 7.4 percent and their profits by 6.9 percent between 1979 and 1980, non-reformed enterprises saw their output *reduced* by 3.15 percent and their profits by 7.39 percent.[30] A whole set of related questions followed. Should the advantaged enterprises be even more favored? If so, why? To give the experiments a greater chance of success? Or was it the *yangzhang biduan* strategy ("develop merits and avoid shortcomings," i.e. use one's comparative advantage) that the Chinese authorities were following in their new economic drive? If so, can the reforms still be called experiments or are they the implementation of a dual enterprise management system, i.e. the *xiaogai* on one hand, and the *zhonggai* and *dagai* on the other? Would this not create inequalities towards the workers in the *xiaogai* enterprises, and what would be the resulting political price?

The other fundamental question regarding these experiments is: Can the right of self-management and, even more, enterprise profit and loss responsibility really be implemented in China? Here questions of basic socialist political economy are engaged, stemming from the central role the industrial sector plays in the development of a socialist system. How much of the tight control exercised by the State over industry could feasibly be relinquished? What should the enterprise's new economic, political and social roles be? If efficiency is stressed through the measure of profits, is there a greater chance for China's economy to revert to some elements of capitalism? How should responsibility, power, authority and benefits be shared among the State, which represents the whole of the people, the enterprise and its workers? Is enterprise profit and loss responsibility feasible when the State owns its assets and exercises such a pervasive control over it? What should the State do if an enterprise keeps on sustaining losses? In such a case, should the State allow it to terminate its operations and, thereby, render its workers unemployed?[31]

In March 1981, the Chinese authorities decided to freeze the number of enterprises taking part in the *zhonggai* and *dagai* experiments and not to expand them to the entire country. From the brief description of these experiments, and the results and problems they generated, one realizes that the Chinese people are genuinely looking for ways to improve their national economic performance and to lower their previous ideological barriers. Yet, this does not mean that they are free from all sorts of ideological and political constraints. In fact, one can reasonably expect that such constraints will become more noticeable in the future, particularly if many of the problems mentioned above are not properly addressed and solved.

Postscript

The implementation of enterprise management reforms in China turned out to be far more complex than the Chinese leadership had expected. The system of enterprise profit and loss responsibility was to be the operations norm for all enterprises in the early 1980s, moving enterprise management systems further down the road of reform. From the very beginning management reforms faced a variety of serious problems, a selection of which are mentioned.

Power over enterprises still entrenched within various government offices and bureaus at the central and local levels, and the bureaucratic net in which organizations have been entangled for decades in China turned out to be major stumbling blocks for enterprises attempting to exercise their newly acquired autonomy. Enterprise management could not exercise the degree of autonomy and initiative the reforms bestowed on them, at least on paper, to be able to operate within the framework of the enterprise profit and loss responsibility system.

Serious systemic problems such as extremely poor distribution channels, semi-protectionist regional economies and markets and a yet-to-be-reformed pricing system have all contributed to the highly imperfect market mechanisms enterprises were expected to operate in when not producing for the plan. Since a sizeable number of enterprises in China were pressured to increase substantially their production for the market, they faced serious problems which have adversely affected the management reforms.

Local governments, whose autonomy had been expanded thanks to administrative decentralization initiated by the central government, increased their grip on enterprises, seeing them as an important source of revenues. Typically, they kept adjusting local taxes on enterprise revenues to siphon off any increase in net profits due to better management performance. This action defeated the purpose and spirit of the profit and loss responsibility system. Moreover, local Party and government leadership's commitment to push enterprise management reforms varied widely across China.

In 1984, the central government stated that a second stage of the profit and loss responsibility system was to be implemented beginning in 1985. That was a euphemism for a second attempt at reintroducing or strengthening the responsibility system already in place. Of course, based on the previous four years of experience, the government reinforced that "second stage" with new or modified regulations.

Progress in enterprise management reforms in China should not be underestimated. Despite the many stumbling blocks the reforms have faced, a sample of which has been mentioned above, management of enterprises has never exercised such a high degree of autonomy and has never been in such a position to operate within market mechanisms since China's socialization of her industry in 1956.

To the Party and government, the rationale for enterprise management reforms implies that control over enterprises should be indirectly exercised mainly through economic leverage rather than directly through administrative measures. For enterprises to respond effectively to economic leverage presupposes the presence of adequately efficient market mechanisms, which has not been the case in China. This situation has resulted in behaviors and performances of enterprises different from those the government expected, and is putting tremendous pressure on the authorities to restore some administrative control over enterprises. If they give in to the pressure, enterprise management reforms will be set back. Removing China's serious systemic barriers to the reforms is the only possible way to have the reforms move forward.

3

Conducting Research in China

Purpose and Scope of the Research

Few studies dealing with Chinese enterprise management have been published outside China, due principally to the lack of access to data and, until recently, the impossibility of conducting fieldwork to research the subject. Studies that have looked at enterprise management in Mao's China fall into two categories. The first is the political science approach to the study of China's bureaucracy and various state organizations. Works such as Franz Schurmann's *Ideology and Organization in Communist China* (Berkeley, 1968) and Stuart R. Schram's (ed.) *Authority, Participation and Cultural Change in China* (Cambridge, England, 1973) are good examples. None of these studies claimed to focus on enterprise organization and management, let alone micro management practice, although they touched on these topics incidentally.

The second category of studies is that dealing with enterprise management directly. Barry M. Richman's *Industrial Society in Communist China* (New York, 1969) and Stephen Andors's *China's Industrial Revolution* (New York, 1977) are two representative examples. The first work was the result of responses to questionnaires the author had submitted to a few Chinese factories (a coup in itself) just prior to the Cultural Revolution. Richman's purpose was to assess the environmental constraints on China's industrial and business management, using the model developed by Farmer and Richman.[1] The second work was based on archival research and dealt with the political management of industrial enterprise.

In addition to these two categories, some studies of the Chinese economy and economic system have touched very marginally on enterprise micro management. Alexander Eckstein's *China's Economic Revolution* (New York, 1977), and Audrey Donnithorne's *China's Economic System* (London, 1967) are examples.

It is clear that none of these authors were in a position to look at Chinese enterprise management on the micro level. There were simply no opportunities for them, to enter a Chinese factory (or any organization for that matter) and observe and collect data that would have permitted the conduct of such a study. A less direct approach to this type of research was likewise impossible, since archival resources and publications coming out of China rarely dealt with the subject. Those studies that did only treated questions of enterprise political management, as did Andors (1977) and Brugger (1975). These books were useful as background information on the subject, but were not a substitute for researching enterprise micro management per se.

A useful source of information about a country's enterprise management is the body of books and materials used there in teaching that subject. Granted, these materials might not reflect management as practiced in enterprises. Yet, as preferred practice, they shed an invaluable light. A more detailed account of the history of management education and training in China follows in chapter 4. For our purpose here, it is sufficient to note that the formal teaching of management as an academic subject had a burst of life in the second half of the 1950s for the first time in the history of the People's Republic. As quickly as it had come to life, it disappeared under a heavy ideological cloud for close to two decades beginning in 1958. Only in 1978, in post-Mao China, was it reestablished formally. Clearly, such a short life, and, more importantly, the ideological black mark with which the field had been branded, were not conducive to the development of teaching materials. Still, some were compiled for use in the few remaining teaching programs in accounting, finance and economics. These programs trained an inadequate number of individuals to work in these fields in government offices and large enterprises.

Even the best of these materials, which were designed for senior college level since no graduate program existed before 1979, were very general and theoretical, with a strong ideological flavor. They introduced the field of enterprise administration in terms of the most basic concepts and functions pertaining to the implementation of economic plans at the enterprise level. No attempt was made to indicate to the student how managerial decisions were made in any of the functions presented, nor how these functions were linked. These materials were more like blueprints of what constituted approved enterprise administration as shaped by the politico-economic parameters at the time. The idea of choice, and therefore risk, that enters into management was not even mentioned. These materials were not only inadequate, in terms of quantity and quality, to acquire any serious understanding of management at the enterprise level, but also, being classified as "restricted circulation," they were normally unavailable to outside researchers.

This situation began to take a turn for the better in the mid 1970s. Scanty, firsthand information on enterprise micro management in China began to reach the outside through foreign technicians and managers who worked in China for short periods as part of trade deals that involved transfers of technology. Typically, they were involved in turn-key plants in the beginning and more recently, in a variety of other arrangements, such as compensation trade, joint ventures, factory management consulting, and the development of management education programs. The latter involved the preparation of case studies and the undertaking of management projects in factories and other organizations. Although these more recent developments have brought about substantial improvement in the opportunities for outsiders to observe Chinese enterprise management firsthand, one must also be aware of the great limitations these outsiders have faced. In a very real sense they have been given the opportunity to see only a few carefully selected portions. To what extent one could interpret accurately what goes on in other sections is debatable. With the reestablishment of programs for the study of management, and the general rehabilitation of management education in 1978, textbooks and other teaching materials have been developed. In 1980, some of the materials began to appear in bookstores, with the quality far surpassing that of the materials compiled previously.

My own residence in China, and involvement in one of these management education programs from its inception, gave me the rare opportunity to experience Chinese management practice from within. Consequently, the emphasis of my research is micro management rather than macro management. Aspects of the latter have already been studied quite intensely by others and are included in this research for the immediate period following the death of Mao Ze-dong. The research technique that I use, participant observation, is a novel one in the study of Chinese management. Clearly, that approach was made possible only because of the recent increase in opportunities for outsiders to cooperate in management studies with Chinese colleagues.

Obviously the limited scope of this book does not allow a comprehensive study of Chinese micro management. Nor can one assume that such a study can be accomplished effectively by any single individual. In view of the present state of knowledge and understanding of Chinese enterprise management, I chose to: 1) emphasize events that I observed or in which I took part that shed light on management practice; 2) place the study of management practices in the context of early post-Mao policies, economic and management reforms, and the Chinese society at large; and 3) analyze those parameters that appear to play a key role in influencing Chinese management.

The two aspects of management practice on which the balance of this study concentrates are: 1) *Management education:* I briefly review the history of management education in the People's Republic, then report case studies illustrating efforts in early post-Mao China to revive this academic field. An analysis of the cases examines the more serious problems, as well as strengths, that surfaced. 2) *The transfer of computer technology into an organization:* Following a brief introduction to the state of the Chinese computer industry and data processing, two cases are presented, one in greater detail. This analysis highlights the technical and, more specifically, managerial problems that Chinese organizations have encountered when introducing the use of computers in their daily activities.

Distinctive Characteristics of Participant Observation

Participant observation, an ethnographic technique, differs substantially from traditional techniques of studying management. First, the researcher is *directly involved personally* with the subjects under study, living within their community or coming into frequent and sustained contact with them. Second, the researcher adopts the *role of a learner* in the relevant community since that community is usually alien to the researcher. Third, the researcher's relationship with subjects under study is usually *complex, long-term and diffuse*. The researcher comes into contact with them in a variety of contexts, such as at home or work, during recreation time, in religious and other ceremonies, and so on. Fourth, in addition to being an observer, the researcher frequently participates to a varying degree in community life, thus becoming a *participant observer*. Fifth, the *researcher does not always control relationships* with the subjects. During the learning phase, such control is probably in the hands of one's "teachers." Because of the long-term and diffuse nature of the relationship between researcher and subjects, the degree and direction of control constantly change. Sixth, when one actually begins fieldwork, the research *lacks specificity and construct*. Only after the necessary period of familiarization with the community under study can the researcher begin to frame specific issues for study. Seventh, the researcher uses a *cyclic iterative process*, rather than a linear one, in collecting and recording information, in analysis and in reporting. Each cycle makes the researcher think of new questions, either to widen the inquiry or to narrow it down and deepen it. This narrowing down of an inquiry is also called the *"funnel approach."*[2]

From this brief presentation of the main characteristics of participant observation, one can see that it puts the researcher in contradictory situations. One pursues both breadth and depth simultaneously. One makes friends but is also a stranger within the community under study. One is both involved and detached. The researcher conducts inquiries both in a "humanistic" and in a scientific mode and holds both subordinate and dominant positions in relations with the subjects.

Participant observation is most suitable to the study presented in this book as the brief discussion of its characteristics above shows. It allowed me to immerse myself within the Chinese society to learn more about it and about the context in which the data presented in this study developed. It has also allowed the collection of extremely detailed information and the close observation over long periods of time of decision-making processes within Chinese organizations. Thus, the presentation and analysis of the case studies and other firsthand data in the next three chapters would have been difficult, if not impossible, without the time-consuming but rich participant observation approach.

Although my principal method is participant observation, this book is not an ethnographic study. This is not the study of a bounded, delimited cultural system, e.g., an African tribe, bus riders, or policemen, with the objective of examining its language, kinship system, social network or behavior. It is the examination of a number of the management questions mentioned above, using an ethnographic approach to data collection. The object of that examination is dual: to acquire further understanding of these management questions per se and to link those management practices to the larger framework of post-Maoist policies and reforms.

Data and Methodology

The research data come primarily from participant observation—both the data on post-Mao policies and enterprise management reforms and on micro management practices. A variety of primary written sources supplement this approach.

Insofar as written materials go, it should be noted that data for the study of social sciences in China are notoriously difficult to obtain and to check. The researcher has to piece together painstakingly the little data available in the Chinese media, both written and broadcast. No data bank exists in China similar to those to which one is accustomed in the West. Also, access to the country has been limited. Only recently have academic delegations, usually within the framework of exchange programs, had the opportunity to visit China. Despite the brevity of their visits, and the limitation on the Chinese host's ability or willingness to provide quality data, many of the delegations and individuals have brought back valuable, though limited and often biased, information which complements that found in Chinese sources, principally the media.

Since 1978, this situation has changed for the better. The treatment of economic and management issues in the Chinese written media has been more frequent and far more substantial. The State Statistical Bureau, under the State Council, was reinstituted and began to compile and publish data on the economy. The Bank of China has been publishing data on monetary and foreign exchanges regularly since 1979. In 1977, in a country of close to one billion people, not a single economics or management periodical was published for general public consumption. However, with the primary importance post-Mao China has given to economic development, research in economics and management, as well as in other social sciences, has burgeoned. In 1978, the magazine *Jingji Yanjiu (Economic Studies)* resumed publication for the first time since the Cultural Revolution. Subsequently, other magazines in economics and management and other areas of social science have appeared on the shelves of bookstores. The titles of some of these publications are: *Zhongguo Shehui Kexue (Social Science in China), Jingji Guanli (Economic Management), Social Science in China* (in English), *Shehui Kexue (Social Sciences), Jingji Daobao (Economic Reporter), Jingji Kexue (Economic Science),* and *Zhongguo Jingji Nianjian (Almanac of China's Economy).*

The increase in the number of such publications available to the public, including foreigners, has been accompanied by a similar increase in publication for "restricted" *(neibu)* distribution. These materials include position papers, reports of studies or investigations requested by governmental organizations, summaries of discussions among the upper echelon of leadership, reports of visits by Chinese delegations abroad or of foreign delegations to China, and the discussion of new ideas or new subjects. Although these materials usually present little that can be considered classified information, the Chinese authorities prefer not to make them available to foreigners or to the public at large. One presumed reason for keeping the circulation of these materials restricted is that their content often reflects ongoing, behind-the-scenes debates, which often precede the modification or the setting of official policy. Yet, any Chinese organization with a direct or indirect interest in the subjects may subscribe to them. A resident in China, who can read the Chinese language and is interested in looking at them, may find the opportunity to do so. Also, with the development of better relations with China—be they cultural, academic, trade, journalistic, or other—reports from foreigners have multiplied and become more reliable. In summary, written information about China's economy and enterprise management has made a quantitative and qualitative leap since the end of 1977.

In August 1977, I began a 28-month stay in China. The first year I spent in Beijing as an exchange student in the Canada-China Students Exchange Program. For the second year, I elected to seek work with a Chinese organization in the area of management. In September 1978, one of the ministries hired me as a "foreign expert"—a foreigner with professional training working for the Chinese organization—in Systems Engineering education. My job was to work with my Chinese colleagues in designing and conducting introductory courses in Systems Engineering for over 100 members of that ministry, people with a variety of working experience. The courses were held at one of the universities overseen by that ministry.

Data collected through participant observation reflects the researcher's own personal experience in the community being studied. The data that I consider to be of help to this research are divided into two categories: general and specific.

General Participant Observation Data

The general category consists of data that assail an ethnographer when living within the community, irrespective of the topic of study. These are the data acquired through observation of the communication system (both language and non-language), the society's socio-economic-political structure, the people's daily life, and so on. The process of collecting these data is rarely structured and is effected in ways that range from the conscious and bemused to the osmotic and matter-of-fact. It goes without saying that these data are essential to a participant observation approach to research. They broaden the inquiry and its context, thereby adding to its meaning. They even help narrow the focus of the research down to the range of the researcher's interests.

I collected these data simply by living in China, observing the society and taking part in numerous activities with the people. I had the opportunity to carry on discussions with individuals from all walks of life—government officials, middle-level cadre, academicians, scientists, students, workers, peasants, car drivers, members of the military, clerks, priests, doctors, and sportsmen. They included people of all ages, of all educational levels, and of all political colors. There were those who were in the good graces of the authorities and some who were not, those

Figure 15.   A Broom Becomes a Christmas Tree, Beijing, 1978.
This demonstrates the need for foreigners'
resourcefulness when living in China.
(Photograph by Author)

satisfied with the turn of the political events and those who were not. Topics include questions related to sociology, philosophy, religion, politics, economics, marriage, divorce, death, education, child rearing, health care, the arts, sports, morality, sex (only with a few Chinese who felt comfortable enough to discuss it), and our personal affairs.

Much can be learned about a society from the daily routine of living and by joining in activities with its members. Those activities in which I participated with Chinese included competing in sports, dancing, picnicing, attending wedding receptions, social visiting in our respective homes, traveling within China, eating out, shopping, using public transportation (an interesting experience in itself), playing cards and other games, watching cultural performances and performing myself. Although in the beginning most Chinese felt self-conscious in the presence of a foreigner, with time many regained their naturalness. Taking part in those activities, I was in the position to learn how different individuals acted in variety of situations, how they thought, how they communicated, and what their values were.

The special arrangements laid out by the Chinese authorities for foreigners in general, and for various categories of foreigners in particular, do not encourage social interaction between foreigners and Chinese, although they are not meant to prevent it, nor could they. Also, they limit the foreigner to certain Chinese social and professional circles depending upon the purpose of one's stay in China. For example, the foreigner on a business mission is largely limited to interacting with representatives of the Chinese foreign trade and other organizations with which he or she is dealing, and with employees of service organizations such as hotels, restaurants, travel departments and taxis. The chances of having meaningful social relations with Chinese are practically non-existent. Unlike someone in business, a foreign expert is less limited in this respect. If the expert teaches in an educational institution, he or she interacts with the administration of the unit, with colleagues and with students, as well as with employees of service organizations. The expert is also in a better position to develop social relations with Chinese because he or she works within a Chinese organization and comes in regular contact with the same individuals for an extended period of time.

While in China, I belonged to three separate foreigners' worlds: that of foreign students, foreign experts and foreign trade, though the latter to a lesser extent and only for a period of four months. I was a foreign exchange student, the spouse of a foreign expert, then a foreign expert myself, and a representative of a United States corporation. Such a rare, if not unique, situation put me in contact on a daily basis with various groups of Chinese in basically different sets of organizations with little overlap among them. In each of these three worlds, roles that were played and expected to be played by the Chinese and by me were likewise very different, and consequently so were our relationships. For example, as a representative of a foreign corporation, I had a businesslike relationship with Chinese counterparts, with very little opportunity for social interaction beyond small talk. Although cooperation was required for our relationship to develop, yet the pursuit of each party's perceived interest (e.g., obtaining the best possible trade terms) was primary.

As a foreign student, my daily contact with the Chinese was primarily limited to students, faculty and administration. My relation with students was egalitarian and relaxed, although naturally only after both sides had adjusted to the many gaps—whether cultural, linguistic, or economic—between us. Relations with the administration and the faculty were of course unequal, with the Chinese side having control and being both paternalistic and protective. Little responsibility and initiative were expected from foreign students. In fact, initiative was usually discouraged. In terms of status, I was on the bottom rung of China's foreign community.

As a foreign expert, I was perceived by my Chinese colleagues and members of the administration of my work unit as an equal. Any indications of inequality went in my favor: I was perceived as being professionally trained and willing to contribute to my unit. Unlike foreign businessmen and foreign students who, in the eyes of the Chinese, are in China mainly to pursue their own interests, foreign experts are generally perceived as having loftier intentions: to help the Chinese work units by offering whatever professional abilities they have. So, relative to other foreigners, experts are held in higher esteem. As a foreign expert, my relations with my Chinese students was clearly skewed in my favor. Notwithstanding the many limitations that foreigners face in developing social relations with Chinese, I was in a position as a foreign expert to develop far more meaningful relations than in any other capacity.

Specific Participant Observation Data

The specific data in the specific-general data classification scheme include those relevant to the research topic, in this case Chinese management. Data in this category are of a broad nature and include any information relevant to the study of management, such as its functional aspects (e.g. finance, personnel, and operations management), its environmental aspects (e.g. national economic policy, law and infrastructure), and its other dimensions (e.g. cultural and socio-psychological).

The specific data were collected in the same way as the general data, that is, through repeated discussions and participation. But the discussions in this case were more likely to be held with representatives of industrial, educational, service and other organizations; with members of government departments that dealt with economic and managerial matters; and with academicians and researchers in the management and economic fields. They were held during visits to these organizations, in my office, or in other more informal settings, such as homes or restaurants.

The participant observation approach to data collection was used principally during the second half of my stay in China when I was involved in a number of activities, some of which were: 1) designing courses in industrial and systems engineering; 2) advising Chinese faculty in the preparation of their teaching material; 3) teaching a management course; 4) participating in the selection, purchase and installation of computer equipment; 5) conducting research projects with Chinese students dealing with questions of factory and educational institution management; 6) discussing the development of management education programs in a number of Chinese educational institutions; 7) lecturing on management topics; and 8) acting as a management consultant to a factory. Naturally, these activities gave me the opportunity to learn a great deal about Chinese enterprise management from a variety of people and under a variety of circumstances.

Typically, data of a general nature were not recorded. Specific data were, with little exception, recorded in basically three ways. The more usual record keeping was taking notes. I never sensed that my note taking caused any apprehension or discomfort in my Chinese interviewees, perhaps because my record keeping technology was limited to a pen and a piece of paper, and I was following native practice: quietly reaching in my pocket for my notebook and pen, and starting to scribble. The second record keeping mode was the set of files I have accumulated in the course of my work in China. These data are in a sense the direct product of my "participation," rather than "observation." Finally, when it was not feasible, convenient or appropriate to take notes on the spot, I would record the information from memory at a convenient time, if the data were significant.

The Personal Dimension

In what ways did my background, personality and personal relations with the Chinese affect my research? Because of the nature of the research methodology used—participant observation, data collection, and analytical inductions—it is essential that my background be presented. As a researcher, one has to strive for objectivity. Yet, strictly speaking, it is clear that it is impossible to attain such a goal, since everyone carries within him or her many biases. Also, on a less personal level, the structure, timing and other similar factors of the fieldwork often present the researcher with a set of data that would not be replicated under any other circumstances. This is particularly so when participant observation methods are used. Although it is practically impossible to measure precisely the effects of the biases, what is important is to take those "distortions" into consideration when analyzing the data.

Because my principal technique was participant observation, I faced many of the problems ethnographers encounter when doing field work:

> On entering the coummunity [to be studied], an ethnographer carries more baggage than a tape recorder and a toothbrush, having grown up in a particular culture, acquiring many of its sometimes implicit assumptions about the nature of reality. And within that framework, he or she developed personal idiosyncracies, and later went through some professional training, learning a set of biases about which areas of the human situation were worthy of attention.
>
> As if that were not bad enough, a social category will be assigned to the ethnographer by the group members [of the studied community]. The category may change over time, but one will always exist. As the ethnographer's role is defined and redefined, it will guide group members in their dealings with him or her. Their expectations of what the ethnographer wants to learn—and their decisions about what should be told—will derive partly from their sense of who he or she is.
>
> These aspects of "who you are" deserve some careful thought. They raise problems for ethnographers, and for all social scientists.[3]

Agar (1980) treated the question of "who you are" under three headings: "personality and cultural background," "ethnography and personality," and "presentation of self." I shall use the same headings in discussing the question of "who I am" during my stay in China.

Personal-Cultural Background

As a stranger to the society he is about to study, a researcher is largely unfamiliar with its customs and habits, the intricacies and subtleties of its structure, its ways of communicating verbally and nonverbally, the daily living conditions, and so on. Given such a situation, it is normal that the alien observer uses points of reference and a framework of analysis which he or she has acquired professionally and personally in prior experience elsewhere.

It is not surprising, then, that one falls victim to improper interpretation of some of the observed events. For example, I noticed that many Chinese, including some of the colleagues I worked with daily, tended to take longer-than-allowed lunch breaks by leaving work ahead of time. I soon came to two conclusions. First, organizations had a common management problem: lack of control over their employees' use of time on the job. And second, that by taking advantage of that lack of control, many Chinese workers displayed a low level of work responsibility. Following informal talks with managers and their subordinates, I found that these two conclusions were correct in some instances but not in others. Many of those guilty of long lunch breaks had to prepare lunch for their family, a task far more time-comsuming and complicated in China than in the West.[4]

In light of this situation, what can be said of my two preliminary conclusions, i.e. loose control over employees' time on the job, and low level of responsibility displayed by some of these employees? If one agrees that a distinction should be drawn between those who must cook lunch and those who do not, then it is clear that the second conclusion does not apply to all those guilty of long lunch breaks. As to the first conclusion, I found that management had adopted a flexible approach in implementing the rules and regulations it had set up. In most cases, management knew about the long lunch breaks, and to those who had to rush back home to cook lunch, it often adopted a tolerant, if not sympathetic, attitude.[5]

Another problem is that even though the observer sees an event and interprets it correctly, he may register different reactions to it or impart a different importance to it, depending on his cultural background and past experiences. For example, the dissimilar cultural backgrounds of my wife and myself at times explained the difference in our reactions to observed events. She was born and raised in England, and I, in Lebanon. For instance, brought up in the sanctity of privacy, she was shocked at the Chinese propensity to interfere in the personal affairs of relatives or friends, and amused at the unquestioned respect accorded to older members of the society. Both cultural traits, stemming from the traditional-authoritarian character of a society, are common to Lebanon, and thus not unfamiliar to me.

Ethnography and Personality

Personality contributes to an individual's reaction to uncertainty. Culture shock is caused by the pervasive uncertainty resulting from "the sudden immersion in the lifeways of a group different from" oneself.[6] Individual reactions to this culture shock vary widely, with personality playing a determining role. Two types of reaction are worth mentioning. One is that of the "authoritarian closure—when central premises of existence are strongly asserted and contradictory information from the new situation is denied."[7] Foreigners prone to that reaction tend to establish "enclaves" for protection and support. Another type of reaction is that of the "autonomous man," which allows a high tolerance for ambiguity and uncertainty.

Skilled ethnographers have the second reaction, which is necessary for successful field work.[8]

As expected, I experienced culture shock upon my arrival in China. It was by far the strongest I had ever experienced, a clear indication that the Chinese culture was more alien to me than other cultures in which I had lived. Yet that culture shock was not as severe as I expected, possibly because of the fact that, as a foreign student, I was part of a familiar social and organizational environment, that of a university, albeit a Chinese one. Also, as are foreigners in China generally, foreign students are peculiarly insulated from the locals. Their usual social circles are limited to other foreign students, a few Chinese colleagues, and fewer faculty members.

About a year after my arrival in China, I experienced another culture shock, far stronger than the first. I was "invited to work," i.e., hired by one of the State Council ministries as a foreign expert in the area of management education. Thus, my daily environment changed dramatically. I dealt professionally with educational, governmental and industrial organizations. Also, as a working member of Chinese organizations, I was definitely on the inside, though still very much on the margin. I shared authority, power and responsibility with my Chinese colleagues. I was part of the decision-making process in my work unit, and relied on others, as I was relied upon, in our daily work. Because of the unfavorable conditions management education faced then (see chapter 4), my Chinese colleagues and I worked under pressure and in close cooperation requiring constant involvement. In short, I was facing on a daily basis the Chinese "life-ways," with all their uncertainties, and to a deeper and broader extent than when I had been a foreign student. Thus, because of the new subcultures in which I moved and because of my deeper involvement in Chinese society, I felt a second, stronger wave of culture shock in the second half of my stay in China.

How did I handle this deeper involvement in a society that is, after all, very different from those I had experienced before? Nash (1963) mentioned the "detached involvement" many ethnographers adopt when living in the alien societies that they are studying. It is a dialectical relationship between distancing oneself from the alien society and getting involved in it. The distancing allows the lessening of the constant strain one is under, and presents the opportunity to examine critically what was learned. Yet the ethnographer has to get involved in order to understand that society more deeply, but that involvement may reduce his objectivity, or even stop him from functioning as a social scientist.

In the second part of my stay in China, my involvement as a foreign expert was far more extensive and intensive than that typical of a social scientist studying an alien society. Consequently, I found that I needed to distance myself periodically from the Chinese culture to restore the balance of the "detached involvement" equation. Precious were the rare undisturbed family evenings and Sunday outings.

As a foreign student during the first part of my stay in China, the "detached involvement" equation was also imbalanced, but in the other direction. The organizational structure foreign students faced tended to insulate them as was, I believe, the unspoken desire of the Chinese authorities.[9] To learn about China's culture and society, I sought relationships with the Chinese and tried to develop extracurricular activities that would get me more involved. At that time, I least desired to distance myself from the Chinese culture.

As a foreign expert, I was in a position to learn far more than as a foreign student. But how much did my close involvement in the Chinese society affect my objectivity in analyzing it? If there was a higher degree of subjectivity, how would the knowledge afforded by my involvement balance my possibly reduced objectivity? Does my distancing from Chinese society since leaving China constitute a counterbalancing factor to be taken into consideration? It is difficult to give clear and accurate answers to such questions. Yet it is important to be aware of these considerations when reading this book.

Presentation of Self

> When you begin doing ethnography, group members are going to wonder who you are. They will listen to you and watch your behavior, and they will draw on their own repertoire of social categories to find one that fits you. At the beginning, you will offer some explanation of what your interests are and what it is you intend to do. This initial presentation of self leads us right into the issue of research ethics.
>
> The data-collection situation is limited and neatly bounded. It involves something like an interview or a test, given by someone who is a specialist in that role. Ethnography is not so nicely packaged. People drift in and out of situations. The ethnographer is not always collecting data in interviews. Does one need to identify oneself to have a casual conversation with a stranger about the weather?[10]

In most Western capitalist societies, the existence of a large, amorphous middle class has weakened social barriers and has dulled the consciousness of social hierarchy. By contrast, as a member of a traditional society, a Chinese exhibits a stronger consciousness of his or her own social position and that of others. To a Chinese, one is first a peasant, a worker, an intellectual, a student, a member of the military or a cadre, and one behaves and dresses in conformity with that social category. Relationships among people are often predetermined by the social position of the individuals involved. For example, many young Chinese commented that, when looking for a spouse, they would look for a person with some preferred occupation or social position. There would be disapproval shown of an "unconventional" person wearing clothing incompatible with his or her social position. The individual would be considered either pretentious or overly modest, depending on the case.

In view of the strong inclination of the Chinese to think and act in terms of their own social stereotypes, it is understandable that such a tendency spills over to the foreigners in China. In 1978 and 1979, a Caucasian met on the street in China would be asked: "Are you an American visiting my country?" To the inquirer, the presence of the Caucasian in his country was a reflection of the improvement of Sino-American relations. Or, if the Chinese noticed that the young foreigner spoke the native language, the question would then be: "Are you a foreign student?" Typically, those are the first words used by a Chinese to start a conversation with a foreigner. If, on the other hand, the foreigner is known to the Chinese, he or she is always referred to and addressed both by nationality and status. For example, the foreigner is: a "French student," or "American businessman," or "Japanese expert," or "Mexican diplomat." This indicates a clear attempt not only to fit a foreigner into a set of familiar social roles, but also to conduct their relationship with him within the confines of such roles.

Upon setting foot in China, to the Chinese I was a Canadian student. Their initial attitude towards me was predictable. Upon knowing my nationality, my new Chinese acquaintances would not fail to remind me about Dr. Norman Bethune and the friendly nature of Sino-Canadian relations.[11] Benefiting from the positive disposition the Chinese had towards Canada, I found that my relationship with them started on a good footing. The low position within the occupation hierarchy enjoyed by students in China, however, applied to foreign students as well, who found themselves at the bottom of the social structure of foreigners in China.

In the fall of 1978, I became a foreign expert, and consequently shot up the ladder of the foreigners' social hierarchy. The Chinese authorities conferred on me additional privileges. As to my previous acquaintances, it is interesting to note that some adjusted their relationship with me to reflect my higher status. In general, upon learning that I was a foreign expert, a Chinese on the street would react warmly, often saying: "Thank you for coming from so far away to help us in our modernization."

What social role did I take in China as a participant observer? Since, unlike foreign students, foreign experts have greater opportunities to take an active role in society, more emphasis is placed here on the period during which I was an expert. From the outset I consciously attempted to "remain marginal to the society" that I studied, and to "stand between the major social divisions, not necessarily above them, but surely apart from them."[12] I considered myself an outsider in the society I was studying and it was appropriate that I not become "engaged." This, of course, fitted the expectation of the Chinese, who, for historical and cultural reasons, were sensitive about foreigners' interference and considered them guests in China. Also, although, as an expert, I was a participant, I tried not to forget that I was first an observer.

Admittedly, it was a difficult balancing act not to make commitments while working as a foreign expert. How could this be accomplished when one had to fulfill one's obligations at work, make decisions and implement them? As a working member of an organization, even the most cautious individual may run counter to someone's interest within or outside that organization, knowingly or unknowingly. Yet would my adapting a neutral position be fair to my employer and colleagues, and would it not have negatively affected my job performance and contribution?

Also, I often found myself unwittingly being drawn into real or potential conflicts. Whenever it suited their arguments or positions on a subject, Chinese colleagues would use the foreign expert in one of two ways. They would lobby for an action claiming that, among others, it would benefit the foreign expert or his work. Or they would claim that the foreign expert supported the position or action they were promoting. My speaking for or against it would have put me in a position of active involvement, and would have embarrassed those who had expressed an opposing view. In China, the worst possible offense is to cause a person to lose face in public. On the other hand, would my remaining silent be a better alternative? My silence could be interpreted as tacit approval of the position being advanced or holding back support for those advancing it.

Being a foreign student and later a foreign expert were the only two ways available to me at the time to experience Chinese society firsthand. Authorities in all the units to which I belonged, as well as my close Chinese acquaintances, knew that I was a researcher and would be writing about Chinese management. Their reactions varied from indifference, to amusement, to interest and support in the form of data, but not, to my pleasant surprise, hostility.

4

Management Education in
Post-Mao China

Following ten days of preparatory work spent at a university where one of the very first management course programs in post-Mao China was to be set up, I met the late Mr. Liao Zheng-zhi, then Vice-Chairman of the Standing Committee of the National People's Congress, to discuss this project. At one point, the discussion took the following turn:

—"So what is your assessment of the situation at the University [where the program was to be held]?" Vice-Chairman Liao asked me.
—"I am impressed with the enthusiasm they have. . . ." I started to say.
—"And that's all they have!" he interrupted and burst out laughing.
—"Yes." I answered after a second's hesitation, and joined him in his contagious laugh.

Beijing, November 1978

Analyzing the recent history of China's economic development, the Chinese leadership came by the late 1970s to the unmistakable conclusion that China's economy would have been substantially better off had it been well managed, both on the macro and micro level. In the fall of 1977, "management"—a word that bears a cultural and ideological stigma in China, as we shall see later on—appeared in the Chinese media, first quietly then more boldly. To convince others and provide themselves with the necessary ideological security and legitimacy, management advocates called upon Marx, Lenin and Mao, selectively quoting them at length to prove their support for the use of modern management in developing a socialist economy. In these advocates' views, as long as it fits China's situation and socialism, modern management shoud be used, whether developed in China or imported from abroad and adapted to the national needs.

If modern management was to be used, one of the next logical steps was to train and educate a contingent of Chinese leaders, cadres and youth in the arts and sciences of management. Although Chinese leaders and organizations interested in this question had no practical experience in that field as practiced or taught in other countries, they realized that sizeable investments must be made to develop the necessary human resources to deal with increasingly complex, interdependent, large-scale economic, technological and managerial problems. In their view, an on-the-job training in administrative matters and "redness"—commitment to socialism—were no longer sufficient, though perhaps still necessary.

The objective of this chapter is to examine the state of China's management education as it was in the three years 1977-1979, when the decision was taken to revive this education field and the first stages of implementation took place. To put current management education in perspective, I briefly review its history in socialist China, principally through the case of the Harbin Institute of Technology. I then consider the major environmental factors relevant to the development of the field and early institution building within the field. A few cases illustrate various aspects of management education: from the debates that were taking place to the implementation of different types of programs. A short presentation of the small but crucial foreign involvement and a brief conclusion close the chapter.

Management Education in Contemporary China

To say that in 1949 China's management education was a "blank sheet" would be wrong.[1] Clearly, the Communist authorities, upon gaining control over the country, wanted to draw a "blank sheet," or at least drastically modify the field to fit the new ideological, social, political and economic order. That this field existed prior to 1949, though in its infancy, is attested by a number of facts. China had a small number of arts and commerce colleges or faculties and schools of business. Business education programs trained students from well-to-do Chinese families in the arts and sciences of trade, accounting and finance. Of course, very little management science or industrial engineering was taught since these fields had yet to be developed. For example, in pre-Liberation Shanghai, Jiaotong University had a business school, and Shanghai College, in the northeast suburbs, was a business school run by American missionaries.

In the early 1950s, with the reorganization of national education, the Chinese authorities had to deal with China's capitalist and Western-oriented business education. The Business School at Jiaotong University was disbanded. Some of its faculty was transferred to other educational institutions, mainly the Shanghai Institute of Finance. The Shanghai College was disbanded, and in 1960 its Western (religious) style campus became the site of the newly established technical college, the Shanghai Institute of Mechanical Engineering. Having swept aside the old capitalist business education system, Chinese authorities began to establish a series of courses or programs that were more attuned to the newly established order. At Jiaotong University, beginning in 1953, attempts were made to offer courses in enterprise organization and management, and in industrial economics. Other more serious efforts were made in Chinese universities and colleges, as illustrated by the case of the Harbin Institute of Technology presented below.

A few of the business faculty were allowed, usually under controlled conditions, to continue teaching and researching. Others had to switch educational fields, or professions, or to undertake ideological reeducation. Most of the faculty that were educated abroad in business, finance, industrial management and other management areas were not allowed to teach in their field for close to three decades, from the early 1950s until the late 1970s. Many had professional training at the masters or doctoral level that made them extremely valuable and scarce, yet untapped but ideologically tainted resources in China. Other untapped resources in management training have been the ex-capitalists, mainly in industrial and commercial Shanghai. Clearly, a large number of these ex-capitalists were unwilling to cooperate with the Communist authorities; some, in time, were. Many fled the country. Yet the often new, inexperienced administrators perceived the ex-capitalists' offers to help in what often used to be their own enterprises as suspicious or threatening. Also, even when they were allowed a managerial role in the enterprise, the ex-capitalists' mode of operation, actions and advice, though possibly economically realistic, were often perceived as ideologically unacceptable. This, of course, substantially reduced the ability of the ex-capitalists to transfer their management expertise to the new administrators.

Following one of the Communists' favorite sayings: "Destroy the old and build the new," efforts to establish management education programs were made across the country starting in 1952. Two types of narrowly defined management programs were set up. The first type trained cadres in applied economics, finance and accounting, and upon graduation, they worked as economic administrators in central and local government economic organizations, performing tasks that varied from drafting economic plans to interacting with enterprises on a daily basis. Management education at Zhongguo Renmin Daxue (China's People's University) represented this type of program. The other type of program provided technical and managerial training in the management of industrial—typically, manufacturing—enterprises. One such program at the Harbin Institute of Technology is described below.

Programs of either type were set up in China following closely, if not copying outright, similar programs in the Soviet Union. For example, the Jilin Institute of Technology in Changqun, Jilin Province, trained engineers and technicians who, upon graduation, worked mainly in factories manufacturing agricultural machinery. When in 1955 the Institute established the "Economics, Organization and Planning of Industrial Enterprise" specialty, it copied its curriculum from the management program at the Moscow Tractor Institute.

The Harbin Institute of Technology

The Harbin Institute of Technology (HIT), situated in the industrial city of Harbin, Heilongjiang Province, in China's Northeast, is one of the country's top engineering schools. In 1978, it was designated a "key" university (see chapter 1 on the recent changes in education policy).[2] Like many other engineering universities, it did not come under the direct jurisdiction of the Ministry of Higher Education. It belonged to the then Eighth Ministry of Machine-Building, which was responsible for the production of tactical weaponry such as cruise, air-to-air and surface-to-surface missiles, and high precision, technically advanced systems and instruments such as missile-guidance systems, instruments and meters for space navigation and lasers. HIT prided itself on having been the first college in China to establish the specialty in management education called "Organization, Planning and Economics of Machine-Building Enterprises." This is not surprising, since this specialty was copied from the Soviet Union, whose political, cultural and economic influence in China, for historical and geopolitical reasons, was most felt in the Northeast. As the name indicates, and characteristic of the Soviet Union's education system, the specialty was narrowly defined in its application, i.e., machine-building enterprises, and its functional scope, that is, the management of this type of enterprises' operations.

The period before the Cultural Revolution: 1954–1966.   After a year of preparation the specialty of "Organization, Planning and Economics of Machine-Building Enterprises" was formally inaugurated in September 1954. In 1955, HIT also established the specialty of Power Economics. The original Chinese faculty that started these two programs were mainly older people who had had teaching or industrial experience in these two fields and a few younger faculty who had recently returned from abroad with university training in these fields. The Chinese faculty worked under the guidance of four associate professors from the Soviet Union, whose expertise was in power engineering management, industrial engineering and economics, and production organization and management. These four Soviet advisors helped establish curricula and teaching laboratories, and taught courses. After 1956, when they left HIT following a stay of two years, management education at HIT developed without the further direct participation of foreign advisors.

In the fall of 1955, HIT inaugurated its Engineering Economics Department, which included the two management programs. Both the teaching and research in this department progressed rapidly in the 1954–58 period but slowed rather drastically between 1958 and 1962. This corresponded to the decline of the technically-oriented Soviet model of enterprise management in China, and to the ascendency of the Communist Party's role in the enterprise's policy making and operations. Following the readjustments in China's education field after the Great Leap Forward, in 1960, the Power Economics specialty was transferred to the Beijing Hydropower Institute, and the Organization, Planning and Economics of Machine-Building Enterprises specialty, to HIT's Department of Mechanics. The Engineering Economics Department was abolished. Subsumed under the Department of Mechanics, the remaining management specialty could not properly be developed.

In 1962, with a more propitious political climate—stressing a more rational, technical approach to economic development in the Readjustment and Recovery period (1961–65) following the Great Leap Forward-the Engineering Economics Department was reestablished. In addition to the pre-1958 activities of the Organization, Planning and Economics of Machine-Building Enterprises program, the new Department offered a Management Executive Program for the training of enterprise management cadre. However, despite serious efforts to return to the hey-day of the 1950s, and after initial successes between 1962 and 1964, management education at HIT faced increasing opposition, which reflected national debates regarding China's economic and education policies and, in turn, enterprise management system and management education. Starting with the Socialist Education Movement, which began in 1962 and reached its height in 1964, conditions for the development of management education deteriorated seriously until the breaking point in mid-1966, when the Cultural Revolution was launched.

The Organization, Planning and Economics of Machine-Building Enterprises specialty had a five-year undergraduate program. Introductory courses in management and economics were not taught until the fourth and fifth years, while the rest of the curriculum was basically that of a mechanical engineering, or more accurately a machine-building engineering, program. Between 1954 and 1966, about 450 people graduated from this program. Upon leaving HIT, most of the graduates worked in factories in cadre positions dealing in planning, production, technical innovation, labor, finance and general administration. Most of these managers ascended to leading positions in factories. Some took up technical and engineering positions rather than managerial ones. A few became instructors in educational organizations.

In addition to the undergraduate program, and during the same 11-year period, HIT undertook the training of 50 instructors who took up teaching positions in programs similar to HIT's in colleges across China. Also, 30 graduate students were trained, and some of them remained at HIT to teach and conduct research. HIT sent a number of people for further training in the Soviet Union in the second half of the 1950s.

At its height, the program had a faculty of 36 instructors. Three research groups were established: the Production Organization Group, the Industrial Economics Group and the Accounting and Statistics Group. The 30 members of these three groups researched questions related to engineering economics, industrial management, cost accounting, financial management of the enterprise, and factory operations management, more specifically production planning, factory layout and production flow, and standardization.[3] As a resource for teaching and research, HIT established a reference room.

July 1966 to April 1978. This period spans the Cultural Revolution and up to 18 months following the removal of the Gang of Four from power in October 1976. The Organization, Planning and Economics of Machine-Building Enterprises specialty and most of the members of its faculty came under strong attack from the beginning of the Cultural Revolution. In 1967 it was the first of any education program at HIT to be officially abolished. All its activities stopped. By 1970, the majority of its faculty were undergoing ideological reeducation in the countryside, and many of them suffered severely, both psychologically and physically. By 1972, with the internal political scene less polarized and less violent, most of the faculty returned to HIT; however, none worked in his or her previous academic field. Some switched to politically less sensitive technical fields, such as precision instruments; others took up administrative positions within HIT; and the rest were transferred to other organizations.

After April 1978. With the new post-Mao economic and educational policies, mentioned briefly in chapter 1, management education was once more considered desirable by the Chinese leadership. The decision to reestablish it at HIT was made in May and June 1978. The first major concrete action HIT took towards the implementation of this decision was the appointing of a task force, the ''Office of Enterprise Management Modernization Studies.'' This office, which went into operation in September 1978, had a dual purpose: to prepare for establishing the education program and to set up research projects.

This time HIT decided to establish a management program, which it called Industrial Engineering (*Guangli Gongcheng*). This decision was taken following a study of similar education programs abroad and in reaction to the narrowness of applicability of the Organization, Planning and Economics of Machine-Building Enterprises specialty and to its heavy tilt towards mechanical engineering. In 1979, HIT's intention was to establish a program with less emphasis on engineering training and more on applied mathematics and applied computer science. It was felt that such a program would prepare its students to deal with management problems in industrial enterprises rather than only in machine-building factories.

In March 1979, the Industrial Engineering Specialty was officially established. It included a reference room and five research groups: Production Organization, Engineering Economics, Operations Management, Systems Engineering, and Operations Research.

Three education programs have been set up under the Industrial Engineering specialty. The first is a four-year undergraduate program, which started in 1979 with 25 students. Based on the list of courses (cf. appendix 1 for the complete listing), the purpose of the program seemed to be to give the students a good undergraduate training in applied mathematics, applied computer science, economics, management of industrial enterprises, and basic mechanical engineering. The other two are executive training programs: one a month and a half long, the other six months long. Each of these two programs was run once in 1979 for a class of 50 enterprise directors and deputy-directors.

In the view of members of the Industrial Engineering's faculty at HIT, conditions for establishing this management program were not as good as in 1954. They mentioned as negative factors the low level of general and technical education following the Cultural Revolution and the older age of the students, who were not used to studying. On the faculty side, in the fall of 1979, only a third of the original pre-Cultural Revolution faculty joined the new 30-member Industrial Engineering faculty. Others wanted to come back to HIT but faced administrative obstacles to their transfer.

HIT's leadership considered that its industrial engineering faculty was old (average age was around 50 in 1979) and possessed an outdated knowledge of industrial engineering from the late 1950s. The faculty was perceived as lacking knowledge of economic theory, principally micro-economics, both capitalist and socialist, of modern economic concepts such as opportunity cost, and of applied mathematics and applied computer sciences, both essential to modern management education and practice.

From reading the little available literature, the faculty had become aware of the latest developments in management education abroad. Yet it was confused by what it was learning. For example, it was not clear as to the differences among industrial engineering, management science, systems engineering, systems analysis, engineering economics and other similar fields, and the areas of their applicability. Consequently, it felt that it was in a difficult situation for establishing new management education programs.

Although aware of the managerial problems that existed in Chinese enterprises, the faculty felt that it could not yet apply new management techniques and expertise in solving them. Also, it felt that the first courses it taught in 1979 were too bookish since most teachers lacked any practical experience in modern management. However, a high level of enthusiasm was present among the faculty and students, and HIT's leadership hoped that this might partly offset the difficult work environment that everybody faced.

HIT's plans were to train its future faculty by taking in graduate students and preparing them for future teaching and research. Its intention was to admit two graduate students in the fall of 1979 and from 10 to 30 in 1980. Also, HIT leadership felt that, with the university's background in engineering and computer science, it was in a good position to establish a Management Information Systems specialty. Its short-term hope was to set up an Industrial Management Department, and its long-term one, a school of management.

Environmental Factors—A Selection

The Harbin Institute of Technology's experience in developing the field of management education is representative of the trials and tribulations this field had gone through in Mao's socialist China. However, HIT was fortunate in that it had provided management education for a longer time than other similar institutions and enjoyed material, financial and staff conditions that were above average in China.

Despite HIT and other higher educational institutions' efforts to train people in management, their impact on China's tremendous need for trained managers has been barely perceptible. Explanations for these mediocre results may be sought in the inadequate amount of the already scarce resources allocated to management education in particular and to education in general. Or blame may be put on the adoption, somewhat indiscriminately, of the Soviet professional education approach that divided management education and training into highly compartmentalized, narrowly defined specialties. Or one may fault traditional Chinese pedagogy, which allows little initiative and practical training for the students, placing more emphasis on the acquisition of knowledge than on developing an analytical mind. Or we can point to an old traditional socio-cultural trait of China which, in marked contrast to current Western societies, ranked management and business occupations very low in the hierarchy of professional pursuits, well below officials and scholars.

Yet, probably the most important factor that explains the lack of success in China's efforts to train managers is politico-cultural. The teaching and practice of modern management have been perceived by a large proportion of Chinese leaders and cadre as carrying with them the definite possibility of introducing foreign capitalist modes of operation into the enterprise. The rationale was that this field has been principally developed and practiced in capitalist countries and reflects their economic and political systems. Consequently, many Chinese shied away from a career in management. More than one management educator confided to me that the principal reason for having a heavy load of engineering course instruction in management undergraduate programs was to give a dual professional training to the students so that they would have the flexibility of practicing the politically less sensitive technical profession, should the pendulum swing again. Wary of potential attacks, authors writing on management-related questions typically quote socialist ideological leaders such as Marx, Engels, Lenin and Mao. At times, this has been carried to the extreme. For example, in the "Financial Management" chapter of a 210-page textbook entitled *Industrial Enterprise Management,* all 29 footnotes attributed quotes to Mao Ze-dong.

When the Communist Party gained control of China's mainland, its experience in economic management was limited to running the economies of the guerrilla bases. Industries in these rural bases were principally handicraft industries, the management of which was clearly different and less complex than that of the more modern urban industries.

In the early 1950s, to remedy its lack of experience, the Party looked for help to the Soviet Union, modeling China's economic and enterprise management after its "socialist brother."[4] The Soviet enterprise management system featured "one-man management" (*yizhangzhi*)—a director with enlarged executive power, who answered to the government department above the enterprise rather than to a body representing the Party. The attempt to introduce this model into China was finally put to rest after much controversy and resistance. Many factors contributed to the rejection of the "one-man management" system. They included China's lack of personnel who combined professional training and loyalty to the Communist Party (i.e., both "red and expert") and the unwillingness of the Party to let the control of enterprises fall into the hands of technocrats. Consequently, since late 1956, the Party has had its own cadres in charge of enterprises, in one form or another. The problem is that in most cases, these cadre are not well versed in technical and managerial matters.[5]

There was also a cultural factor that played an important role in the rejection of the "one-man management" system. Giving too much prominence to one individual in the enterprise, i.e. the director, rather than stressing the collective leadership went against the norms of proper behavior in China, particularly if that individual was younger than his colleagues. This would have been the case had China implemented the "one-man management" system for which a younger generation of "reds and experts" would have had to be trained. Also, the long tradition of officials administering the Chinese Empire, and the emergence of the Chinese "bureaucratic capitalist" industry before 1949, had created bureaucratic rather than managerial modes of running the economy.[6]

In summary, in the 30 years of the People's Republic, China seemed not to have been in a position to design, develop and put into place a modern enterprise management system that would be socially and politically acceptable, as well as culturally and economically feasible. The Soviet and Western management systems were rejected for cultural, environmental and ideological reasons. In their place, the Chinese developed various versions of enterprise management, which afforded an important role to the Party. These have turned out to be too politicized and inefficient in the view of the current Chinese leadership. The country's inability to settle on its own enterprise management system, which in essence can be done only through a political process, has not allowed management education to develop in China.

By 1978, the management legacy in China was considered by the Chinese leadership to be very backward. Surveys conducted in post-Mao China showed alarming results for a country that wanted to modernize its economy. In 1979, only 20 percent of top managers of industrial and transportation enterprises in industrially advanced Liaoning Province, in China's Northeast, had had any professional training. In Shanghai, of the 2,000 production management cadre of 64 key enterprises of the First Bureau of Electrical Machinery of that municipality, only 16, or 0.8 percent of the sample, had graduated from higher education institutions. The First Ministry of Machine-Building conducted a survey on the formal education level of the top leadership of 249 of its key enterprises. Of the over 2,400 cadre at the directorship level, 64.3 percent had an elementary or junior high school education, 21.4 percent had a senior high school or secondary technical school education, and only the remaining 14.3 percent had a higher level education. Also, the majority of the university-trained cadre had technical rather than managerial training.[7]

The samples of these surveys were biased and nonrepresentative of the country as a whole. Liaoning Province and Shanghai are economically and managerially more advanced than the rest of the country. Also, in all cases, the samples included key enterprises, which had priority over other enterprises in the allocation of human resources. It is highly probable that were a national survey conducted on the formal education level of the management in Chinese enterprises in 1979, the results would have been even more shocking than those cited.

Clearly, the formal education level of a manager is not a sufficient assessment of management ability. Personal characteristics including abilities to relate to others and to lead, professional experience and on-the-job education should also be taken into account, among other factors. But a lack of professional training in a technical, managerial or economic field is definitely a great handicap for a manager trying to operate in the increasingly specialized, technical world of enterprise management. Needless to say, this handicap is more severe if the manager lacks a high school education.

The low level of enterprise management in China was also reflected in the rarity with which enterprises adopted some basic modern management tools and techniques. During the Great Leap Forward and shortly thereafter a serious attempt was made to introduce basic operations research techniques and methods in a few key enterprises, but this effort could not develop properly due to the political upheavals of the Cultural Revolution.[8] Since 1979, that attempt has been revived. For example, many economic and management magazines, typically *Jingji Guanli (Economic Management),* have contributed to the popularization of modern management techniques and methods by presenting in each of their issues articles and examples on the basic applications of Linear Programming, P.E.R.T. and other similar, quantitatively oriented management tools.

Institutional Building

To raise management training and practice to a level more in line with the new economic drive, the country's leadership took a series of decisions and actions concerning the fields of management education, training and research. In the fall of 1977, the Institute of Philosophy of the Chinese Academy of Sciences split away from the Academy to form the basis of the newly established Chinese Academy of Social Sciences. One of the five economic research institutes that soon became part of the new Academy, the Institute of Industrial Economics established in 1978, was interested in researching China's industrial economic structure and its management system.[9] This interest included the study of the national enterprise management system from an economic point of view, and of the micro-economics of the enterprise. Soon, the Institute started to publish the results of its research, including a detailed assessment of the management of the Daqing Oil Company and a monthly magazine, *Jingji Guanli (Economic Management),* the first issue of which appeared in February 1979.[10]

In mid-1978, two management research associations were established under the Chinese Association of Science and Technology: the Chinese Research Association for Modern Management and the Chinese Research Association for Engineering Economics (or Technology Economics).[11] The principal objectives of these two associations were to facilitate the introduction from abroad and adaptation to China's needs and environment of management theories, techniques and expertise, to promote their development domestically, and to popularize their use among Chinese organizations. Soon after their founding, both associations began addressing the field's theoretical and methodological questions; establishing communication networks among research, education, government and industry organizations; developing human resources in the field; and undertaking projects for the dual purpose of training people and of demonstrating the positive results of properly applying modern management techniques. The Chinese Research Association for Modern Management was more interested in the application of management science, systems engineering, systems analysis, operations research and other similar techniques for improving industrial operations within a sector (e.g., adoption of industry-wide standards and rational development of an industry on the national or regional level) and within the enterprise. The Chinese Research Association of Engineering Economics' professional interest was in the application of these management techniques to the technical and economic study of large-scale projects.

In March 1979, the China Enterprise Management Association was founded under the sponsorship of the State Economic Commission. Its stated purpose was to study "questions of industrial, transportation and capital construction enterprise management," and the "theories, systems, techniques, methods and experiences of domestic and foreign enterprise management."[12] The Association was active in conducting executive training programs and conferences, in publishing and circulating professional materials, in establishing links with counterparts abroad, and in conducting practical experiments in enterprises. Its close relationship with the

State Economic Commission has made it an increasingly influential professional organization.

Other professional societies, usually of more narrowly defined interests, have been established in the field of management since 1979. To name only a few: the Society of Economics of Capital Construction, the Society of International Trade, the Systems Engineering Society, and the Association of Textile Enterprise Management. The purpose of these societies, like the others described above, is to promote the understanding and application of modern technology and management techniques and knowledge in the sectors of interest to them. These societies would sponsor conferences, executive training programs, and the publication of books and materials, and would establish a domestic as well as an international communications network to facilitate the circulation of professional information within and into China.

These societies were established because of the need to address problems within a certain field, as recognized by prominent people in governmental, industrial and intellectual circles. The idea of founding a society was usually initiated by one such person or group of people, who would then act as its sponsor. For example, Kang Shi-en and Yuan Bao-hua, then respectively chairman and vice-chairman of the State Economic Commission, were closely involved in the founding of the China Enterprise Management Association; Yu Guang-yuan, then vice-president of the Science and Technology Commission, of the Chinese Academy of Social Sciences and of the Chinese Association of Science and Technology, in the founding of the Chinese Research Association for Modern Management and the Chinese Research Association of Engineering Economics; and Qian Xue-sen, vice-chairman of the National Defense Science and Technology Commission, in the founding of the Systems Engineering Society. The involvement of people of national stature legitimated these societies and enhanced the power of their founders to secure scarce resources.

In addition to the efforts of the professional societies to promote management training and practice and to coordinate the activities of interested organizations, a large number of academic institutions joined in the revival of management education, executive training and research. In academia, two approaches to the development of management teaching and research programs were followed, principally determined by the structure of China's higher education system.

The first approach was that of the then Ministry of Higher Education, which had the overall academic responsibility for China's higher education, set general standards and requirements for all Chinese universities and colleges, and directly supervised a large number of higher education institutions around the country. Since the Ministry's interests were broad and cut across sectorial and professional training, its efforts in developing management education were not limited to training managers for a particular type of enterprise, as HIT's Operation, Planning and Economics of Machine-Building Enterprise specialty had been. They tended rather to encourage wide coverage of the field and to include the implementation of academically more rigorous programs that could lead to graduate studies and the training of researchers in the future. Consistent with the clear academic distinction between economic and financial management on the one hand and enterprise industrial management on the other, the Ministry took a parallel, yet distinct, approach to the development of these two types of management education. As an illustration, let us take a brief look at the Ministry's effort in the second type of management education.

In late 1979, the Ministry of Higher Education sponsored the "First Conference of Industrial Engineering Specialty in Engineering Higher Education Institutions Under the Ministry of Education." The conference was held in Shanghai at Tongji University. Among the Ministry's universities that took part in the conference were Tianjin University, Tongji University, Qinghua University, Central China Institute of Technology, Dalian Institute of Technology and Xian Jiaotong University. These six universities were considered among the best technical education institutions in China, reputed for the quality of their graduates and their research. The Ministry also invited other universities to take part in the conference. These universities, which were not directly under its jurisdiction but had all established industrial management courses or programs, included Shanghai Jiaotong University, Shanghai Chemical Engineering University, Shanghai Institute of Mechanical Engineering and the Harbin Institute of Technology. The following questions were discussed: objectives of industrial management education, curriculum design, management executive training, and the need to establish joint projects between universities and enterprises.

A follow-up meeting was held in early spring of 1980, during which it was decided that the six universities under the Ministry would establish industrial engineering programs and that Qinghua University would act as the coordinator. The objectives of these programs were to train industrial engineers in a combination of engineering and managerial skills so that they could act as consultants on, or work in, planning and control, production management, engineering economics and management of technology in enterprises. In addition to their undergraduate programs, the six universities were required to train graduate students, with the goal of establishing graduate programs. This was in line with the Ministry's responsibility for training high caliber personnel to develop teaching and research in this management field. These universities were also required to hold management executive training and refresher courses, principally for cadre who possessed a technical or managerial training background. They were one of the best qualified groups of universities to give such courses, the academic and professional levels of which were expected to be higher than other executive training programs in view of the trainees' high education level.

The second approach to the academic development of management education was that of national and local government organizations, which had their own education institutions that trained personnel for their operations. For example, the First Ministry of Machine-Building had 12 universities and colleges directly under its jurisdiction. The number was reduced to seven in March 1979, when the Agricultural Machinery Ministry spun off from the First Ministry, taking five of these universities under its wing. These two ministries' universities trained technical, engineering and administrative staff and cadre, most of whom eventually worked for them. Clearly, they had their own need for training managerial personnel who would work in their administrative organs and in the thousands of enterprises under them. They were interested both in developing academic programs, principally at the undergraduate level, to train managers and administrators for the future, and in setting up management executive training courses for their scores of current managers. In addition to these two ministries, others were also active in the development of management education and training programs. They included, among others, the Ministry of Textile Industry, of Railroads, of Communications and Transportation, of Foreign Trade, and of Petroleum and Chemical Industries, the Eighth Ministry of Machine-Building, Beijing and Shanghai Municipalities, and the Bank of China.

Because of their large number and the urgent need to train their own managerial staff, these universities were far more active in management education development than were those of the Ministry of Education, although the latter were more visible and prestigious both in China and abroad. Other factors set them apart from the universities under the Ministry of Education. For instance, belonging to industrial or commercial industries, from which management training demand originated, they were under tremendous pressure to design and conduct management executive courses for millions of their own cadre. The majority of these courses had to fit with the cadre's low formal educational level, stressing ideological and policy issues and briefly introducing the trainees to the problem areas in which modern management techniques might be put to use. Of principal interest in the undergraduate program was the training of a young generation of managers who combined a knowledge of management with that of the industry technology with which they would be expected to work, such as machine-building or banking. Naturally, while such training did not have the narrowness of the pre-Cultural Revolution management specialties, it was more specific than that typically provided by the Ministry of Education. It tended to train individuals in management techniques, methods and tools for immediate use rather than in a broader disciplinary approach.

Debates and Plans: Industrial Engineering Specialty Conference— Qinhuangdao, Summer 1978

At this early stage of the development of management education, all institutions mentioned above were facing the same basic issues. They were defining the scope of their activities and of the management education field of direct interest to them; and they were translating their perceived need for management education programs into action against an environment characterized by severe scarcity of resources including information. Let us remember that these issues were faced after more than a decade of severe attacks against this field. To help us appreciate better the issues and environment faced then, let us briefly look at the case of the First Ministry of Machine-Building.

The First Ministry of Machine-Building sponsored the Industrial Engineering Conference which took place in the resort city of Qinhuangdao, Hebei Province, in the summer of 1978.[13] Two similar conferences had been held in China before. The first one, held in 1952 soon after the Communist takeover of China, established a number of educational programs in industrial management and industrial engineering specialties and subspecialties such as the Organization, Planning and Economics of Machine-Building Enterprises at the Harbin Institute of Technology. The second conference, held by the First Ministry in 1964 in Hangzhou, occurred after the readjustment and recovery period that followed the severe problems of the Great Leap Forward. At that time, a revival of management education was attempted amid controversial political debates, including the question of what management system China should have. This attempt was unsuccessful and short-lived since the Cultural Revolution was launched in 1966.

The First Ministry of Machine-Building was the largest of China's ministries that dealt in engineering and manufacturing. Unlike the other machine-building ministries, its products were normally allocated to the civilian sector. A wide range of manufacturing industries came under its jurisdiction, including the heavy machinery, machine tool, generator, boiler and automotive industries. It supervised more than 8,000 factories and had about three million people on its payroll.[14] It had its own administrative structure, which penetrated all layers of government at the county and township levels and above. Also, the First Ministry had built up a number of auxiliary services to help it perform its main manufacturing activities. For example, it ran its own network of hostels to provide accommodation for its members on business trips within China. It had its own education system that spanned the range from day care centers to higher level education institutions. It had set up a number of research institutions, technical information centers and libraries. It sponsored professional organizations such as the National Mechanical Engineering Association. Thus, it is not surprising that the First Ministry would take the initiative in holding a conference on industrial engineering and promoting the development of this field in China.

Over 100 people, 50 of whom were educators, took part in the Qinhuangdao conference. They came from various departments of the First Ministry, from more than ten higher education institutions, some belonging to the First Ministry, and from other interested organizations. The conference agenda was broad and ambitious. It included determining the type of management education programs needed to train high level technical-managerial personnel for the thousands of factories the First Ministry supervised; adopting a unified plan to set up management-related courses at its various colleges, and, more particularly, to establish management education specialties in three of its colleges; and planning a series of management executive programs to begin soon which would involve at least one member of the top executive leadership of 800 of its most important factories.

Three topics seem to have taken center stage at the conference: directions in the development of industrial engineering; curriculum planning and development for the undergraduate programs in industrial engineering in technical colleges; and discussion of programs and teaching materials for the plant director executive management training course.

The participants came away with a degree of clarification, though no total agreement, on the types of management education programs China and, more specifically, the ministry needed. A draft of an undergraduate industrial engineering curriculum was produced, although it did not receive unanimous approval. Teaching materials compilation groups were established for both executive training and undergraduate programs. A preliminary plan for implementing the executive training program was drawn up. A number of universities worked out detailed plans to establish or reestablish management education programs. The Mechanical Engineering Management Association was founded under the National Association of Mechanical Engineering, itself sponsored by the First Ministry. It was decided to undertake a feasibility study for the establishment of an Industrial Engineering Institute.

A more detailed look at some of these decisions provides an additional understanding of the state of management education and its environment in China. Participants in the conference recognized the need for two major types of management education programs: economic management and industrial management. In their view, institutes of finance and economics should provide economic management programs to train cadres to work in central and local government organizations. They would constitute the body of technocrats who would manage the national economy on a daily basis. Engineering and technical colleges should offer industrial engineering programs to train high level technical cadres to run industrial enterprises, and manage engineering, research and development and economic analysis projects. While participants agreed on the need for these two types of education programs, they were divided on which of the two programs should be stressed. As one might expect, participants from institutes of finance and economics argued for economic management programs; those from engineering and technical colleges for industrial engineering programs.

A draft of an industrial engineering curriculum was worked out. Articulated at the conference by Sun You-yu, then vice-minister of the First Ministry, one of the basic philosophies underlying the draft was that, unlike in the 1950s and 1960s, the engineering and management training in the industrial engineering program should be wide and versatile to prepare students to deal with a variety of engineering and management problems rather than with a narrowly defined application area.

The draft of the industrial engineering program suggested a four-year undergraduate program consisting of 2,500 to 2,800 hours of instruction. A number of points distinguished it from previous management education programs in China.

Emphasis would be put on training in applied mathematics such as probability and statistics, operations research and linear algebra, and in computer science applied to engineering and management, neither of which had been part of management education in the past. Also, the draft suggested that China ought to learn from a variety of sources about modern management techniques and experiences, rather than from a single source, which had been the Soviet Union in the 1950s and 1960s. The content of the management courses must be selected based on its practical applicability to China, rather than on its theoretico-ideological base or on "empty principles." Likewise, students ought to be introduced to ways of applying what they would learn through projects. Participants at the conference also stressed the need to eliminate the overlaps in the management courses that had existed in previous management programs in China.

The curriculum itself (see appendix 2) seems to be composed of four major parts: courses in basic sciences common in engineering programs; courses in machine-building engineering; courses in industrial engineering; and practical training in the form of three projects. It is interesting to note that the engineering courses, which seemed from their titles (e.g., Metal, Materials and Heat Treatment, and Machine Tools and Cutters) to be narrowly limited to machine-building, were supposed to provide the desired engineering training in the program. On the other hand, without knowing more about the content of the management courses, it is difficult to assess whether the management training part of the program would turn out to be narrow or versatile. The practical nature of the training was indicated not only by the requirement of three different projects in the course of a four-year program, but also by the requirement that, to graduate, a student complete the "technology design" and the "product organization design" projects.

A number of questions related to the design of the industrial engineering curriculum were debated but not resolved because of the diversity of opinions. Here again the question of the mix between economics and finance courses, and management techniques courses was discussed. The share of the curriculum allocated to management courses was also debated. Some argued that, to provide adequate training in management, the program ought to have as many management related courses as the draft of the curriculum had. Others argued that the share of management courses ought to be reduced, presumably for more engineering courses. Many thought that the confusion might have been caused by the participants' uncertainty about what modern management was, what the curriculum of a modern management education program should include, and how best to train students in this field. It appears that not much time was devoted to this question despite the need to clarify it. Also, many would have liked to discuss the distinctions among systems engineering, management science, engineering economics, industrial engineering and other management fields, the nuances of which had puzzled many a Chinese scholar and government official.

A number of decisions were made during the conference regarding the First Ministry's management executive training program. As mentioned above, the ministry wanted at least one member of the top executive management, if possible the director, of each of its 800 most important factories to enroll in one of the training courses in that program. Three types of trainees were expected: the veteran directors, typically put into positions of power after the Chinese Communist Revolution, usually possessing little formal education but a lot of administrative experience, and considered more "red" than "expert"; the newly promoted directors who had a better formal education, usually technical; and those who had military backgrounds and had been offered this civilian position upon retirement. The conference participants estimated that over 80 percent of the trainees would have a low level of knowledge and might find it difficult to digest the course materials.

It was planned that a number of training sessions would be held over a period of three years, beginning in 1980, to cover those 800 factories. Each course would take 50 to 80 executives and would last from three and a half to six months. The six colleges that were assigned the task of offering these courses were: Shanxi Mechanical Engineering Institute, Jilin Institute of Technology, Hubei Agricultural Machinery Institute, Tianjin Institute of Finance, Hebei Mechanical and Electrical Engineering Institute, and Hefei Institute of Technology. Each of these colleges was to help compile teaching materials in fields that included: political economics and economics theory, industrial economics (including concepts of industrial efficiency), enterprise management, statistics and other quantitative methods, and introduction to computer applications to management. The instructors would come from these and other colleges, and from factories and government organizations. When necessary, trainees would have to enroll in basic courses before participating in the executive training courses.

Management Executive Training Programs

Some of the most important and acute problems enterprises have been facing in post-Mao China were described briefly in chapters 1 and 2.[15] A whole set of factors were at the root of these problems, ranging from an overconcentration of power in central political organs to the adoption of a seemingly inadequate worker incentive system. Also, as the results of surveys of the education level of enterprise directors, mentioned earlier in this chapter, indicated, China faced a severe lack of skilled managers. This problem was compounded by China's commitment to a renewed economic drive, for which a large contingent of capable managers was needed. Thus, it was no surprise that the Chinese authorities emphasized the urgently needed management training of cadre, rather than the education of the next generations of young managers through long-term academic programs. This tactic was expected to have a more immediate effect on improving enterprise management. Moreover, since most of the Chinese universities establishing management courses or programs had to start from scratch, it seemed easier to implement short executive training programs than academic programs.

In terms of content, level and the audience they addressed, there were two categories of executive training programs. The first, closer to those discussed at the Qinhuangdao Conference, addressed the training of cadre who did not possess a higher education, its equivalent, or managerial or technical training. The trainees in this category constituted by far the majority of China's economic cadre and typically had a political or military background. The training programs in this category took a number of forms. Some were a series of lectures that the cadre attended on a part-time basis. Others required the full-time participation of the cadre, who then took time off work. They lasted from a few weeks to a few months, reflecting among other things the variation in the breadth and depth of these programs.

Their curriculum varied, yet they had a number of common points. A heavy emphasis was put on ideological and political economics instruction, principally to clarify in the mind of the cadre the theoretical and practical significance of post-Mao economic policies. Also covered were recent developments in technologies relevant to the economic sector of interest to the cadre, and the application of modern management methods and techniques, including the use of applied mathematics and computers, to solve managerial problems. This served mainly to inform the cadre of major developments in these fields and alert them to the benefits of modernizing their operations. In some cases, cadre were required to take a battery of basic remedial courses such as linear algebra before joining the management training program.

Typically, these programs were in-house; that is, the enterprise itself or a government organization above it would design and conduct them. For example, Anshan Steel Company, China's largest iron and steel complex, possessed its own educational facilities up to the tertiary level, employing 1,740 teachers and staff in 1980. Three hundred ninety of its factory directors and party secretaries rotated through a two-and-a-half-month training course in the first half of that year.

Unlike the Anshan Steel Company, most enterprises did not have adequate resources to offer cadre training programs. In those cases, such programs would be designed and conducted under the ministry or other government organization that supervised the enterprise. For instance, the Qinhuangdao Conference discussed plans for such cadre training programs for the First Ministry of Machine-Building's key enterprises, as mentioned above. These programs were to be developed by representatives of six universities under the supervision of the ministry. (See appendix 3 for a sample of a curriculum outline of one course of this type.)

The second category of management executive training programs addressed the training of those cadre who had had a higher education or its equivalent in technical or managerial fields. Compared with the first category, the ideological and political economics content in this category of programs tended to be lower. The treatment of technology and management subjects was more technical, deeper and more sophisticated. The purpose of the training was to teach the students about recent developments in modern management and show them how to apply management techniques and tools relevant to their enterprises. These students, typically mid-career professionals, were expected to join their enterprises' in-house group of experts, to take an active part in the introduction and practice of modern management in their enterprises, and, in turn, to train some of their colleagues in this field. The duration of these courses varied from a few weeks to six months.

Unlike those in the first category, these courses tended not to be offered in-house but rather on a national or regional level, probably because of the high level of instruction required. Organizations that provided such training courses were the national professional societies, universities under the Ministry of Education or other high level government organizations. Also, research institutions were occasionally involved, whether under the Chinese Academy of Sciences, the Chinese Academy of Social Sciences or other national government organs.

A brief outline of the first of such programs offered by the Chinese Research Association for Modern Management will illustrate this category. Following a period of researching and designing the curriculum in 1979, in early 1980, a few months after the first anniversary of its foundation, the Association announced that it would conduct a graduate course in modern management. The course was to start in April of that year and last for a month and a half. The announcement proposed lectures on theoretical and methodological questions of modern management, quantitative methods, management techniques and computer applications to management. Also, discussions on special management questions including the rational use of existing resources were planned. The association's selection criteria were: candidates must be management cadre, engineers or technicians who were dealing in management or planning at the level of a factory, government department and above; they must have a university degree or the equivalent; and they must be sponsored by their work place. The association reserved the right of final selection.

The course lasted from April 12 to May 26, a period of over six weeks. The following is a sample of the courses offered: Linear Programming, P.E.R.T. and Graph Analysis of P.E.R.T., Quantitative Methods in Economic Comprehensive Analysis and Plan Balancing, Decision Theory, Integrative Systems Engineering for the Optimum Design of Production Management, New Methods in Optimization, and Computer Languages and Applications. Also, during the course, most students attempted to relate their studies to management problems they were facing at work, and some worked on models or methods to solve them upon return to their work units.

Taking part in the course were 140 students, who were deputy-chief engineers, engineers, research associates and university instructors. They came from ministries, commissions and research organizations under the State Council, and from higher education institutions. Their average age was 43. All 140 students reportedly performed well, and their average mark was over 90 points. Only 134 students graduated, since six returned to their work place before the end of the course due to urgent business.

Because it was offering one of the first such urgently needed technical courses in post-Mao China, the association was in good position to select its students from among China's most technically qualified mid-career engineers, managers, researchers and instructors. Presumably, they were both "expert" and "red," since they held high level positions in their work units, which had sponsored them for the course. The high caliber of the students contributed to the success of the course. Also, the course benefited from the attention of high level government officials at the ministerial level, many of whom discussed the possibility of establishing a similar course within their own ministries. To provide the necessary high level instruction, the association enlisted the cooperation of some of China's most qualified researchers and teachers in applied mathematics, applied computer science and industrial engineering. Soon after the course ended, the association held a second, longer session in August 1980. That session was sponsored by the Ministry of Textiles, which sent by far the largest contingent of students. The content of the course was basically the same as in the first session, with more emphasis on relating the materials to the textile and other light industries.

The efforts begun in 1978 to upgrade the professional level of the nation's cadre resulted in the training of five million cadre through short courses for the three-year period of 1979 to 1981. The training covered not only managerial instruction, but also vocational, technological and even basic knowledge. In 1980 alone, 730,000 leading members of industrial and transportation enterprises took management training courses: 328,000 (or 45 percent) of these trainees came from 4,400 enterprises that were taking part in the enterprise management reform experiments (see chapter 2). Fifty percent of large and medium-size enterprises ran training courses for their workers, staff and cadre. Some of these courses included management instruction. Ministries dealing in industry, transport and communications, as well as 13 provinces, municipalities and autonomous regions, ran full-time management programs and provided short-term training classes. The authorities planned to continue this effort to train Chinese cadre. The national objective was to have every cadre in industrial organizations receive managerial and technical training by 1985. Also, the authorities emphasized the training of managerial cadre in the 30- to 50-year-old age bracket, deciding to provide the younger generation of management graduates with the equivalent of a management internship in a commune, a factory, a school or a county.

Two other significant events were closely related to the overall upgrading of enterprise management education in China. On March 3, 1979, the day the Chinese Enterprise Management Association was officially founded, the first Enterprise Management Graduate Course of the State Economic Commission run by the association was inaugurated. The students were heads of the State Economic Commission branches of China's provinces, municipalities, regions and large industrial cities, heads of some of the largest and most powerful enterprises, and leading cadre from industrial, transportation and communications organs of the State Council. They were among the most powerful cadre dealing in national economic management, more particularly in the implementation of China's economic policies and plan. Then Vice-Premier Kang Shi-en gave the inaugural speech and Yuan Bao-hua, then vice-chairman of the State Economic Commission and newly appointed president of the association, directly supervised the course. The content of the course was divided into three parts: basic socialist economic theory; economic and enterprise management systems and their reforms; and foreign countries' experiences in economic and enterprise management. The lecturers were among the most prominent members of China's intelligentsia who designed post-Mao economic policies in China. A selection of the lectures offered during the course was edited and circulated in China (see appendix 4 for its table of contents).

The second event of importance to upgrading management knowledge in China was the development of two series of television lectures on industrial economics and enterprise management under the title "Basic Knowledge of Enterprise Management." The lectures, which were broadcast over a period of three months beginning in late May 1980, were sponsored by the All-China Federation of Trade Unions, the Central Television Broadcasting Company and the editorial board of *Jingji Guangli*. The ten lectures on industrial economics dealt with contemporary issues in this field in China. For example, the issues of industrial economic reforms, of the combination of planned and market economies, and of importing technology were covered. The lectures on enterprise management addressed basic functional areas of enterprise management, such as the management of labor, materials, equipment and the plan, and introduced the viewer to the use of computer and systems engineering in this field (see appendix 5 for the titles of the two series of lectures). The purpose of these lectures was to popularize basic economic and management knowledge among China's cadre and to show the interrelationship among various economic and management fields. The public reaction to these lectures was highly favorable. It was estimated that over two million people saw the first airing of these lectures. The lectures were published, and soon the 1.8 million copies were sold out. Hundreds of organizations requested copies of the films for in-house showing and study, and local television stations rebroadcast selected lectures.

Academic Programs in Management Education

Parallel to, and in conjunction with, the development and implementation of management executive training programs, efforts to establish academic programs started in selected higher education institutions as early as mid-1978. Typically, these were the institutions that had had management education programs prior to the Cultural Revolution, when the field and those involved in it were subject to fierce attacks. One such institution was the Harbin Institute of Technology, mentioned above. Soon, a surprisingly large number of colleges and universities began to develop management education, many of which, like the prestigious Qinghua University, had no recent experience in this field. This rush by higher education institutions was prompted by the Chinese leadership's recognition of the importance of modern management to China's economy, and by the resulting directives from government organizations rapidly to develop academic programs to train China's future managers and management educators. The Ministry of Higher Education and the First Ministry of Machine-Building typify this situation, as we saw above.

All the universities and colleges that received such directives faced a difficult task regardless of their past experiences. As described earlier in this chapter, the field had been banned from the education system in China from 1966 to 1978, and had been under attack for close to a decade beginning with the Great Leap Forward in 1958. By the late 1970s management education in China lagged far behind its counterpart in Western countries. In other parts of the world, particularly in economically developed countries, the field had progressed at an impressive rate. Many Chinese in positions of leadership, particularly those who were members of one or more of the hundreds of Chinese delegations that have been abroad on study tours since 1978, considered China's gap with the West in management techniques and expertise wider than its technological gap. Compounding the problem, China, as a developing country with one billion people, lacked adequate resources to allocate to the development of this field. These two pervasive factors must be kept in mind at all times when studying management education in China, particularly academic programs, which require long-term commitment and sizeable investments, both of which tend to be neglected in the face of pressing short-term problems. A case study of the development of one such program follows.

Development of Management Academic Programs—A Case Study

In mid-1978, a large industrial ministry decided to train two groups of its employees from across the country in computer science and systems engineering for management. It commissioned one of the universities it supervised to develop the training programs and conduct the courses.

The university had grown from a technical vocational school to become an engineering college in 1960. Upon graduation, its students usually worked for organizations belonging to the industrial ministry that supervised it. Developed using the Soviet education approach, the university was organized along five or six narrowly-defined specialties in electrical and mechanical engineering. Its four-year curriculum emphasized education in the basic sciences and mathematics, and a narrow technical training in the chosen specialty. The teaching of social sciences and humanities at the university was limited to three courses required in all tertiary education programs across China: Political Philosophy, Political Economics and the History of the Chinese Communist Party. The first two courses introduced the student to Marxist philosophy, ideology and economics. In 1978, the university offered no other courses in social sciences or humanities. This curriculum is not atypical for technical and engineering colleges in China.

The ministry set up two classes at the university in the fall of 1978: the Computer Science Refresher Course (*Jisuanji Jinxiuban*) and the Systems Engineering Refresher Course (*Xitong Gongcheng Jinxiuban*). Thirty-two people, whose age averaged in the mid-30s, took the first course. They came from 24 organizations, 2 of which were research institutions and the other 22, engineering colleges. Thirty-eight people, averaging 40 years old, took the Systems Engineering Refresher Course. Their educational and professional backgrounds, though technical, were more diverse than the first group's. They came from 29 organizations: 12 research institutes, 11 engineering colleges and 6 factories. For both courses, the students came principally from organizations belonging to the ministry, most of which were not considered first rank education or research institutions.

The principal objective of these courses was to give the students a basic foundation in their respective fields. The first course trained students in computer systems (hardware and software) and programming, the second course taught concepts of systems engineering, including computer systems software and programming. All students were expected to return to their work units, where they were to introduce the field of their training, mainly by teaching it. The courses spanned two terms: the fall-winter and the spring-summer semesters. In the first term, they covered foundation materials in mathematics (calculus, linear algebra, probability and statistics), computer sciences (principles of computers, principles of programming and programming languages) and graph theory. In addition to the common curriculum, each course covered additional topics specific to its field. The Computer Science Refresher Course offered courses in electronics and systems hardware and software. The Systems Engineering Refresher Course offered a course in control theory.

About the time the university was to conduct these courses in the fall of 1978, the ministry decided to hold a third course: the Systems Engineering Teacher Training Course (*Xitong Gongcheng Shiziban*). This course was scheduled for the spring-summer semester (February to July) of 1979 and was to be set at an academic level substantially higher than the two other courses. The purpose of the course was to train 38 lecturers in systems engineering for management purposes. The academic and teaching background of the students was principally in the physical sciences and engineering. Their age averaged in the late 30s, and they came from 19 organizations through a selection process that was supposed to use stricter criteria than those used for the first two courses. With the exception of one research institute, all the organizations that sent students to the course were universities, almost half of which were not under the ministry's jurisdiction and at least one third of which were considered among the top universities in China. In a sense, the teacher training course was the first national project for the training of mid-career academics in modern management techniques in post-Mao China.

With the exception of a few subjects, the ministry and the university decided to consolidate instruction for all three courses—the two refresher and the teacher training courses—for the spring-summer semester. Administratively, however, the three courses were kept separate to reflect differences in their objectives and in the professional level of their trainees.

The course subjects covered in the spring-summer semester overlapped with those covered in the fall-winter semester, particularly in the area of computer science. The university considered this overlap beneficial to the students in the refresher courses because the level of instruction was higher and the subject coverage was more comprehensive in the second term than in the first. Courses in principles of computers, in programming languages including BASIC, COBOL, FORTRAN and ASSEMBLER, in operating systems and in data processing systems design and analysis were offered. The management science component of the instruction was covered by courses in systems analysis, operations research, modeling and simulation, control theory and graph theory.

Most of the instructors who taught the refresher courses in the fall-winter semester were from the university. Others were invited to lecture from other educational institutions. On the other hand, the caliber of the students and the intended high level of instruction in the teacher training course necessitated that most of the lecturers come from outside the university. In the spring-summer semester, for all three courses 14 instructors were from the university, 23 came from 12 other research and teaching institutions, and one engineer from an electronics factory. One foreign expert and 9 administrative and support staff took part in the courses, all located at the university. Nine of the 12 outside teaching and research institutions had been recognized in China as having established an excellent professional reputation. Most of the lecturers from these institutions were considered among the most knowledgeable in their area in China. Typically, their subject was self-taught, and they were engaged in researching it rather than teaching it. It was interesting to note that many of the visiting lecturers and most of the lecturers from the university audited the teacher training course, when they were not themselves teaching it. To many, it was an opportunity to widen their knowledge of modern management techniques and to cooperate with colleagues in this small but growing field in China.

The ministry, through its education bureau, funded the three courses and oversaw their proper conduct. The university had full responsibility for their implementation, in the process of which it enjoyed an adequate degree of autonomy. Clearly, it had to abide by general regulations and guidelines set by the education bureau of the ministry following discussions and negotiations with the university and other interested departments within and outside the ministry. These guidelines included conforming to the objectives of the courses, the proposed curricula, the students' selection criteria, quotas of students allocated to a selection of factories, universities and research institutes, and financial procedures. The allocation of financial resources to the courses was adequate by Chinese standards and comparable to similar professional mid-career training programs in China in 1978-79. But by Western standards, the project was facing an extremely tight budget and required good financial control. Yet had the allocated budget been larger, its marginal utility would have been low, because the two scarcest resources needed for the courses, namely instructors, and equipment and materials, could not be obtained with additional funds.

The university had to scout nationwide for many of the instructors it needed to conduct the courses in the spring term. The two principal reasons it succeeded, as we have seen above, were a network of personal and institutional relationships, and the attention gained by the Systems Engineering Teacher Training course as the first such course in post-Mao China. Only for those two reasons was the university able to arrange the participation of visiting lecturers.

In all cases, the arrangement was struck between representatives from the university and the top leadership of the lecturer's work place. Typically, the university covered expenses, but neither the lecturers nor their organizations were compensated. The visiting lecturers' participation in the course was considered a favor their organizations granted the university or the ministry, and not the result of the kind of business arrangement with which we are more familiar in Western countries. In an environment where qualified lecturers in modern management were scarce, and where securing their participation was more a matter of favor than of bidding for their time, a good network of relationships was clearly vital.

In the fall of 1978, teaching materials for the Systems Engineering Refresher Course and the Computer Science Refresher Course were limited to those that the university lecturers and the small number of visiting lecturers had compiled. These materials covered subjects taught in engineering programs in China, such as applied mathematics, control theory, and technically-oriented—as opposed to applied— computer science. Thus, the compilation of these materials did not present major difficulties to the lecturers in terms of their familiarity with the subject, nor the availability of library resources. However, there were two principal flaws in these materials. First, much of the content of the technical material was outdated, probably reflecting the library holdings at the university and in China in general. Second, the materials were prepared and taught in a bookish form, with undue emphasis on the technical and theoretical at the expense of the practical aspect of the training. Both of these flaws stemmed from the low level of development of systems engineering and computer science in China and from the inadequate professional experience of the lecturers.

In October 1978, when preparations for the Systems Engineering Teacher Training Course began, the university's Chinese and foreign language library holdings for systems engineering, management science and applied computer science were, for all intents and purposes, non-existent. By acquiring teaching materials from engineering and management schools in the United States and Canada, receiving complimentary copies of textbooks from English language publishers, and purchasing books in the United States, the university had established a Systems Engineering Reference Room by the beginning of spring 1979. The materials in the reference room were a substantial, though far from adequate, aid in preparing the teaching materials of many of the university and other visiting lecturers, who could read English. Soon, the existence of the reference room became known to interested parties in China. More outside researchers and teachers used it than those connected with the systems engineering courses.

Despite the tremendous improvement that these up-to-date materials offered lecturers at the university, the use made of them was clearly suboptimal for a number of reasons. Most lecturers and students did not possess an adequate reading ability in English to profit from these materials. Those who did often paid attention to the technical/theoretical content of the materials and neglected their practical content. A number of factors explained this approach, including traditional, Confucian pedagogy, the lecturers' lack of practical experience in applying their course subjects, which strengthened the traditionally bookish approach of teaching in China, and the ideologico-political climate at the time. The last factor can be best illustrated by the decision made by many lecturers not to use problems and exercises found in the North American materials on the grounds that they reflected Western, capitalist economic systems rather than the Chinese, socialist one. More specifically, some of the lecturers in quantitative methods for management refused to use problems that addressed profit maximization. Such caution on the part of the lecturers must be understood against the background of the long history of the political trials and tribulations of management studies in China, and in the context of the political uncertainties of post-Mao China as perceived by many intellectuals in 1979. After all, many a cadre had paid dearly for suggesting that profit play a role, however minimal, in the management of enterprises. On the other hand, suggestions made by the foreign expert to adapt the problems to China's ideological and political climate, such as turning the problem from an exercise in profit maximization to one of production cost minimization, remained only suggestions.

In the spring term, at least four courses in computer language programming and one course each in computer operating systems and data processing were offered. To be effective, the teaching of these courses and of most of the courses in quantitative methods for management should have required the students to use computers. Yet the university's computer facilities comprised two small, second-generation computers, whose lack of external memory and adequate system software and peripherals limited them to the equivalent of programmable calculators and ruled out their use for the systems engineering courses.

In December 1978, the university acquired a DJS-130, a third-generation small mini-computer, whose mainframe was copied from a Data General mini-computer that was marketed in the U.S. in the late 1960s. The DJS-130 that the university obtained had no external memory, no operating system, and no software, nor, in some cases, hardware interfaces with its peripherals. The students were able to use the DJS-130 to execute a few programs written in an elementary version of BASIC language only. At the time the systems engineering course was closing, in the beginning of summer 1979, four U.S.-made micro-computers were installed at the university, driving 16 terminals and providing the use of a whole gamut of systems and application software. To all intents and purposes, there was no computer facility at the university, when the Systems Engineering course offered hundreds of lecture hours in computer courses. (See chapter 5 on the implementation of the systems engineering computer center.)

The university succeeded in finding lecturers for all the courses composing the original curriculum of the Systems Engineering Teachers Training course, with the exception of Applied Statistical Analysis, which was not offered. New courses related to systems engineering were subsequently added to the curriculum whenever university representatives identified a person who was recognized as an expert in his field, and who was willing to teach the course. Consequently, a typical weekly class schedule included on average 30 hours of lectures time—with peaks of about 40 hours—and one afternoon of political studies. Thus little time remained for individual study, homework, discussions and computer practice. Students felt that the high proportion of lecture time was justified, and, indeed, desirable, and the majority of them requested to have more subjects added to the curriculum. The university leaders responsible for the course shared this feeling and responded positively to the students' requests whenever possible.

A number of factors explain this emphasis on lectures. Possibly, the most significant factor was the Chinese concept of pedagogy, rooted in the traditional, Confucian approach to teaching, in which the teacher lectures to the students, providing them with the substance of the materials to be covered. The students' duties were to retain the content of these lectures and be able to reproduce it. Students were not encouraged to discover and learn the materials on their own with the teacher's guidance, and to learn how those materials were developed so as to understand their capabilities and limitations. Another factor was that those who designed the curriculum did not appreciate how crucial practical training, through discussions and homework, was. The course could not rely on any precedents or past experience. Finally even if the university and the students wanted to emphasize practical training, the total inadequacy of the computer and other facilities at the university would have not allowed it. Thus, the course was a bookish rendering of basic quantitative tools and techniques used in modern management. (No lectures were given on managerial economics and social psychology.)

The Systems Engineering Teacher Training Course can be considered a first attempt at the long and arduous process of building up modern management academic training programs. As the first step, the course introduced the types of tools and techniques—borrowed from the field of engineering—useful to solving management problems. It did not actually train those future management lecturers in teaching or applying these tools and techniques. Perhaps the university's deliberate attempt at offering the widest possible range of subjects fitted well with its objective of bringing these subjects to the lecturers' attention. Perhaps it was also realistic to set such a limited objective in view of the particularly difficult conditions the university was facing: the scarcity of qualified, experienced teachers, the material environment in which it had to conduct the course (lack of computer facility and teaching materials), the persistent ideological and political handicap the field of management was still facing, and the tight budget on which it was operating.

The Foreign Factor

As we have seen in chapter 1, the Chinese leadership has, since 1977, strongly advocated that China should learn from other countries, particularly those technologically more advanced. The idea was to transfer under the authorities' control scientific and technical knowledge and know-how and adapt them to China's situation for the purpose of its modernization. The science, techniques, know-how and art of modern enterprise management were on the import list, at least according to statements by Chinese media and officials since late 1977.

In the summer of 1978, a year after the Chinese media started its campaign about studying foreign modern management, I offered my services in the field of management education. After considerable preparation and negotiation I became the first management education foreign expert in post-Mao China in the fall of 1978. A few months later, a French citizen became the second foreign expert to teach management in China.[16]

When post-Mao China first opened to the outside world, the Chinese made more effort to learn about hard technologies from abroad than about management—in their eyes a politically value-laden technology. Inquiries about management were made principally in an indirect way in late 1977 and in 1978, for instance, between Chinese and foreign economic delegations in China or abroad. Typically, the Chinese side would report details of those discussions in internal, restricted professional publications, which circulate widely among the middle- and upper-level cadres in China. In some instances, non-restricted Chinese publications would carry articles of a general nature relating to economic and enterprise management abroad.

Gradually, the Chinese also began to request from representatives of foreign companies that they touch on relevant managerial questions when making technical presentations. For example, discussions of manpower organization, quality control and repair and maintenance management would be included in a series of technical presentations on a production process or a sophisticated piece of equipment. This represented a significant change on the part of the Chinese, who had made a point, in most cases of technology transfer, of avoiding open discussion of management questions with their trade partners during the Cultural Revolution. Chinese socialist enterprise management was not to be tainted by its capitalist or foreign counterparts.

In addition to politico-ideological factors, practical factors also inhibited the initial efforts of the Chinese to learn about foreign modern management. All these factors have been alluded to earlier in this chapter, yet it is important to mention some of them here to assess their impact on the early stages of the process of the transfer of management technology to post-Mao China. Foremost among the practical factors was the lack of institutions that could interact with their foreign counterparts in the field of management education. National organizations interested in the development of management education in China did not start to be established until late 1978. For example, the China Economics of Technology Research Society and the China Management Modernization Research Society were established in the second half of 1978 under the China Science and Technology Association. The China Enterprise Management Association was founded in March 1979 under the sponsorship of the State Economic Commission. On the academic level, decisions to establish or re-establish management education programs in universities and colleges were not made until late 1978. Clearly, these fledgling organizations were not in a position to conduct exchanges with their foreign counterparts.

The scarcity of properly trained human resources also hampered rapid and efficient institutional build-up, whether in national societies and associations or in academic schools and departments. Most of those qualified to take part in the restoration of management education as a professional and academic field were also faced with a dilemma. On the one hand, they wanted to practice their profession again, and they were fully aware of the benefits that would accrue from cooperating with foreign institutions and colleagues. On the other hand, they knew that management education and foreign connections have each been notorious targets of political and ideological attacks for long periods in the history of the People's Republic of China.

This dilemma has at least slowed down many an individual's involvement in management education and dealings with foreigners, even when condoned by the Chinese organizations they belonged to. Chinese management experts correctly perceived the lack of consensus within the country on such highly sensitive subjects as how much foreign input the Chinese should tolerate and what sort of management system should be established. Foreign input has always been perceived as carrying potentially serious threats to Chinese ethnicity and culture. Moreover, in a Marxist framework, the question of management systems is highly politicized, since management constitutes an important component of the relations of production in Marxist economic theories. Yet despite that lack of consensus and the political risk it implied, the Chinese authorities desired to explore, experiment with and adopt new ways of managing enterprises, when old ways had not been entirely satisfactory. Yet who knows when the pendulum might swing, leaving many advocates of modern (i.e., foreign) management exposed to potentially damaging criticisms?

A third factor was the initial reluctance of foreign governments, including that of the United States, to make management part of the scientific, academic and cultural exchange programs then under negotiation with the Chinese authorities. The U.S.-China scientific exchange program the Carter administration had in mind initially excluded management. Only at the insistence of the Chinese was it finally included. In the fall of 1979, a Ford Foundation delegation visiting China was willing to offer Chinese scholars fellowships to study a number of fields, including law, in the United States. Yet it was originally reluctant to do the same for management, despite the requests made by their hosts. As in the case of the Carter administration, the Ford Foundation in the end acceded to the wish of the Chinese.

A final important practical factor that explains the slow rate of transferring management technology from abroad was the unfamiliarity of the Chinese recipients and the foreign donors with each other and with each other's management education field. One of the major concerns of Chinese management educators was to obtain up-to-date information on developments in the field since the early 1950s. Also, they needed to acquaint themselves with institutional structures of management education in foreign countries and identify relevant channels for future transfers.[17] Foreign donors had no less of a need to familiarize themselves with the Chinese situation, an endeavor that had been practically impossible to undertake until the opening up of post-Mao China. Before engaging in any meaningful discussions about transfers, potential donors had to learn about the recipients' level of management education, institutional set-up and priorities, among other things.

In 1978 and particularly 1979 Chinese organizations began to consider possibilities for cooperation with foreign counterparts in the field of management education. In those two years, China showed a special interest in learning more about the economic systems and policies and the management of the national economies of a number of countries in Eastern and Western Europe, in addition to the United States and Japan. However, in management education, there was a widespread belief in China that the latter two countries had the most to offer.

It is interesting to note that the structure and delivery of management education differs in the United States from that in Japan. For instance, in the United States, management education is mainly provided in specialized, comprehensive educational institutions, i.e., schools of business and management, which are quite separate from other professional training institutions, such as engineering schools or departments of economics. Such a sharp distinction does not exist in Japan. Also, graduate training, particularly for the Master in Business Administration, is rare in Japan. With its more specialized, structured and focused management education, the United States is probably in a better position to respond to China's desire to transfer management education, at least in the initial stages.

As a first step toward transferring management education from abroad the Chinese began to exchange delegations. Education delegations exchanged between China and other countries in 1978 and 1979 were mostly interested in education in general or in scientific and engineering training in particular. Only in the second half of 1979 did exchanges of management education delegations take place. In July 1979, one delegation from the Alfred P. Sloan School of Management at the Massachusetts Institute of Technology, and one from the Harvard Business School visited China under the sponsorship of different hosts.

Three months later, a Chinese counterpart visited the United States for the first time in the history of the People's Republic. The idea of inviting a high level Chinese management delegation to the United States had originated in 1973 in discussions between Professor Richard D. Robinson and myself at the Massachusetts Institute of Technology. Later that year, an invitation was extended to the Chinese authorities through the Chinese Liaison Office in Washington; it was turned down on the grounds that "It would not be too convenient for a management delegation to visit the U.S. at this time." The door was, however, left open by the Chinese representative, who suggested that the invitation be extended again a year later. The second invitation met with a similar fate. The invitation was extended for the third time in 1978, in the more propitious political climate of post-Mao China. It was accepted, and resulted in the fall 1979 visit.[18]

The case of the first Chinese management delegation to the U.S. is significant to the understanding of enterprise management and management education in China in a number of ways. First, and once more, it supports the thesis that management, particularly the examination of Western management practices and skills, was political in the eyes of the Chinese leadership: the political climate of 1973 to 1975 had not been conducive to such an examination, whereas that of 1978 and 1979 was. Second, the Chinese representative's suggestion that the invitation be extended a second time, though it might have been a civil gesture, also reflected a latent interest in learning about Western management. The political factions harboring this interest chose not to turn down entirely the invitation, hoping for a more propitious time to express it publicly.[19] Third, prior to the Chinese authorities' acceptance of the invitation extended in 1978, many Chinese organizations interested in management competed for representation on the delegation. The fierce competition was a clear indication of the importance of the delegation's visit to the United States. Finally, the Chinese authorities' selection of Ma Hong and Xue Mu-qiao as delegation leader and delegation advisor, respectively, reflected the importance they accorded to the visit, and was tangible evidence of their commitment to examine Western management practices and skills.[20]

The success of technology transfer characteristically rests partly on the initiative of individuals on both sides of the transfer, as well as on the collaboration that develops between them. These individuals act as transfer facilitators.[21] The case of the delegation is significant in illustrating this point. The planning, visit, and follow-up activities for this event would not have taken place in the way and at the time they did without Professor Richard D. Robinson, to a lesser extent myself, and many Chinese individuals, particularly the delegation leadership. Soon after the delegation returned to China, the Chinese public was introduced to management education in the United States with the publication of a book, titled *How the United States Trains Enterprise Management Personnel,* written by members of the delegation.[22]

Apart from formal education delegations, another important channel of information was the visits of numerous management educators to China, either as members of professional cum tourist groups or as individuals. The latter group consisted mainly of ethnic Chinese, returning on a visit to their ancestors' land. Finally, the very few management "foreign experts" working in China formed another channel. Their importance was disproportionately larger than their very small number, as we shall see in chapter 6.

The Chinese had specific objectives for these exchanges. The principal one was, of course, to learn about management education abroad. Many a Chinese group sat listening attentively to presentations made on this subject by foreign educators. In addition to academic degree and executive training programs and curricula, the Chinese were often interested in discussing teaching approaches and other pedagogical questions. The many questions they put to their foreign colleagues indicated their serious desire to learn and reflected the many problems that they had been facing in this field.

Collecting printed materials, such as university catalogs and bulletins, course outlines and syllabi, was crucial to the transfer of the needed information. Such materials were read carefully, consulted repeatedly, translated in part, and widely distributed to interested parties.[23] Management textbooks published abroad began to trickle into China, typically through foreign academic connections. Chinese organizations, which had been allotted foreign exchange book funds, could submit a purchase list of foreign books to the China Books Import and Export Corporation, selected from the corporation's catalog. In 1979, management books were added to the catalog.[24]

The second major objective of this exchange of delegations, materials and information was to allow Chinese management educators to use what they were learning about foreign management education in their effort to build up the field within China. Research and training in that field had stopped entirely over 15 years before, at a time when it was developing at a fast rate abroad. There was a need in China to define the field, its subjects, and the disciplines that underlie it. Also, in the now pressing tasks of designing, developing, and teaching executive training and academic programs, foreign management education became a vital input, along with remnants of the experience and knowledge of the few qualified Chinese management educators. The Chinese seemed to want to use foreign management only as a reference, albeit an important one, and not to copy it. They seemed to recognize the significant differences that set China apart from industrially developed countries, namely its economic, management and education systems, its technological level, the types and levels of needed management training, and the stage of development of its management education, to name a few.

The third major objective was for the Chinese to learn enough about foreign management education systems to begin exploring possibilities for their cooperation with foreign counterparts. It was clear then that the Chinese authorities had approved such explorations but had no concrete ideas, let alone plans, as to what such arrangements should or could be, how to go about establishing them, and with whom. Because of the isolation and barely initiated institutionalization of the management education field in China, 1979 was limited to exploration only. The few agreements reached in that year were loose understandings for the foreign university to accept one or two management students or scholars for further training, for the exchange of books and materials, and for the Chinese university to receive foreign faculty to lecture in China. Exchanges of ideas on what might be more significant cooperative arrangements were initiated. There was talk of a management center to be set up and run, with the United States involved; of an experimental program at the masters degree level, modeled on similar programs in the U.S. and taught by North American faculty; and a Chinese government request to include the field of management in Sino-U.S. science and technology agreements then under negotiation, with the possibility of significant U.S. government support in that field.

How successful were the Chinese in their early attempts at re-establishing contacts with foreign management education circles? In their attempts to learn about foreign management education, the Chinese successfully collected and studied relevant information about programs, curricula, teaching philosophies and methods. A number of factors explain this positive record. Exchange delegations were used efficiently, with excellent groundwork prior to the visits, efficient use of the visit time, and well conceived and focused programs. The general disposition of the parties involved in the exchanges was positive, friendly, and cooperative, particularly at a time when China was entering the international scene with great fanfare and welcome, after a period of semi-isolation. With the repeated encouragement of their leadership, the Chinese displayed positive attitudes and inquisitive minds, conducive to learning from their foreign counterparts.

Much was learned from the seemingly random amd disjointed series of lectures on various aspects of management education given by academics visiting China, particularly ethnic Chinese. The Chinese were able to piece the contents of these lectures together and profit from them beyond original expectations. Notwithstanding a certain degree of competition among themselves, Chinese organizations interested in management education cooperated by sharing information and jointly sponsoring professional activities involving foreign colleagues.

As for the second objective—beginning to use foreign management education materials in Chinese management training programs—Chinese management educators seem to have performed satisfactorily. Whenever textbooks, syllabi and teaching outlines were available, they were used at least as references, if not as major content. The typical approach was to combine the foreign materials with those developed locally, or to adapt them to the Chinese environment and the particular needs of the program. The most useful types of materials were those addressing management techniques, both operations management and quantitative analysis, rather than finance, economics, and behavior and organization sciences, all of which were less suited to the Chinese environment. The use of foreign materials was, however, limited by the instructors' weak, or nonexistent, knowledge of a foreign language. Selected materials, principally textbooks, were translated, yet they did not provide an optimum use of imported materials. The principal limiting factors were the instructors' lack of feel for the field and the vast literature consequent on its development in the last two decades.

Chinese efforts to attain the third objective were comparatively less successful. By the end of 1979 or early 1980, there were few academic exchange agreements that either focused on management education or included it in broader exchanges. The lack of proper financial support and the looseness of the agreements were two principal explanations. While there were agreements to exchange students and faculty, there were no specific plans and commitments for such exchanges. None of the exchanges offered a plan for cooperation between the concerned institutions, nor an attempt to fit the exchanges into an ongoing education program in China. Also, the structure of the agreement and the standard of living differentials left most of the financial responsibility for the agreement to the foreign partner. This seemingly paradoxical outcome may also be explained by the Chinese's perception, or perhaps misperception, of the ability and willingness of the foreign partner to shoulder the financial costs. Carried away by the novelty of, and the possible opportunities that might result from, exchanges with the Chinese, most foreign education institutions entered into those agreements without seriously considering their financial implications. Perhaps these few agreements were premature, considering the stage of the field in China. Yet they might be considered part of the learning process for all concerned.

It seemed that, in addition to the types of exchange programs noted above, the management education field in China would benefit from a more active, better planned cooperation between Chinese and foreign institutions. The transfer of management education programs, designed, packaged, implemented and financed by both parties, would be highly beneficial and probably more effective than the types of exchanges that had already been set up. Such programs would provide a focus and a basis for cooperation between the two parties, and, as pilot projects, a foundation for the design and implementation of similar programs in other institutions in China. In late 1979 and early 1980, representatives of the Chinese and the United States governments discussed the establishment of such a program. At about the same time, representatives of an industrial ministry initiated negotiations with a private U.S. consulting firm to help them design and implement an M.B.A.-type program, with an emphasis on operations management.

The limited foreign participation in management education in China stems from the Chinese authorities' desire to control foreign involvement in their country; from the sheer magnitude of the needs, which cannot possibly be satisfied only by foreign sources; and from the unique features of the Chinese economic and management systems and national objectives, all of which necessitate a primarily local role. Indeed, early attempts at reviving management education have relied almost entirely on Chinese resources. Yet a foreign role is also crucial, inasmuch as it opens vital channels of information, knowledge and know-how, and provides financial and human resources and the benefit of other societies' experiences.

Conclusions

A number of factors recur in various facets of the reestablishment of management field in China. Politico-ideological factors, which were primary to the abolition of the field for two decades, seem to have become positive, if official pronouncements and actions are considered. Cultural factors, on the whole, have hindered the development of the field. Traditionally unfavorable views of the business and management profession persist. The basic values and concepts of modern management conflict with those of traditional Chinese culture.[25] The scarcity of qualified management educators and the pervasive lack of experience are probably the major determinants of the speed and method of developing the field. Yet educators seem intent on defining and developing it rapidly.[26] A weak, though rapidly expanding, institutional infrastructure is another factor. The reliance, to a limited extent, on foreign involvement, with all its advantages and disadvantages, is a final aspect of re-establishing management education in China.

Despite official statements regarding the importance of introducing modern management in Chinese organizations, and of building up management education and training programs, the meager resources allocated to those tasks, compared to the allocation for scientific and technical education, indicate a lukewarm commitment. Similarly, among the thousands of students and scholars sponsored by the Chinese government to pursue their training abroad, hardly any were in the field of management from 1978 to 1980.

Compared with other countries, China has fallen behind in the design and development of management education programs. As noted earlier in the chapter, in the late 1970s and early 1980s industrial engineering and operations management education programs have developed essentially separately from those of business economics and finance. It seems that those programs do not intersect enough to provide an efficient training for upper level and general management. Moreover, both lack a component of behavior and organization studies relevant to the Chinese environment.

The most noticeable strengths of Chinese attempts to build the management education field have been: the ability to compensate for adverse environmental effects and weaknesses with efficient organization and cooperation among various Chinese groups; the strong, though financially inadequate, backing and close cooperation that government organizations have provided; the enthusiasm and dedication of many management educatiors, and an international environment favorable to China.

Postscript

China has made tremendous progress in developing management education in the first half of this decade. Hundreds of management education programs, including executive training and undergraduate and graduate academic programs, have mushroomed in universities, enterprises, professional societies and government organizations. Each year, millions of managers at all levels have benefited from executive training programs, and tens of thousands of students have graduated from management programs, be they industrial engineering or economic and financial management programs.

Any political and ideological stigma put on management education in Mao's China has been removed by Chinese authorities' pronouncements regarding the crucial importance of economic and enterprise management for the country's modernization, and more importantly by their actions supporting the continuous development of the field. This newly revived field is now part of the mainstream of China's education system.

The administrative and curriculum reforms of the education system, the sizeable improvement in education standards and increase in resources allocated to education and the restoration of the prestige of the teaching profession lost in the tumult of the Cultural Revolution have all contributed to the rapid and positive development of management education.

Still, there are a number of problems plaguing the field, all of which have been mentioned in this chapter. The lack of competent teaching staff and of well-developed teaching materials, the high degree of compartmentalization of education even within the field of management, e.g., management and industrial engineering, Confucian pedagogical biases, insufficient resources and inexperience, are still adversely affecting the development and quality of management education. Politically sensitive subjects, such as organization studies, behavioral sciences and marketing, which had not been taught in Mao's China, are absent from many curricula, or inadequately covered.

Foreign involvement in management education has surprisingly been widespread and effective thanks to professional and financial commitment on the part of the Chinese and their foreign counterparts. Though small in proportion to the total efforts expended in China, foreign-sponsored management education programs have played a leading catalytic role, due to their usually high quality students, curriculum design and the mostly foreign teaching staff. They are considered elite programs training elite groups of students and faculty, and are set as models for domestic programs to follow. Programs sponsored by foreign governments—including those of the United States, Canada, France, West Germany and Japan— to the tune of multi-million U.S. dollar annual budgets, have made their impact in China. A variety of other programs sponsored by multinational organizations such as the World Bank or the United Nations, by universities representing most OECD countries and through private foreign channels have been implemented.

The rate of success of these programs and China's tremendous needs for management education have strongly encouraged the Chinese authorities to seek more foreign cooperation to transfer management knowledge and know-how, and to adapt them to suit its environment.

5

Management of the Transfer
of High Technology

China's modern industry, particularly its heavy industry, was founded on the massive transfer of technology from the Soviet Union in the 1950s. Entire industries were set up in China, and others modernized or expanded following the signing of the Sino-Soviet treaty for economic cooperation. The transfer included equipment, materials, blueprints, as well as technical expertise in a variety of forms, particularly in the training of Chinese scientists, engineers and technicians in the Soviet Union and in the presence of Soviet technical and management advisors in China.[1] Comparatively little transfer of technology took place in the 1960s, following the Sino-Soviet Rift and the Cultural Revolution. The 1970s saw another important wave of transfers from Japan and Western countries in selected industries, particularly iron and steel, chemical, petrochemical, fertilizer and machine-building industries.

The transfer of technology undertaken in the 1950s differed from that of the 1970s in a number of ways. In the 1950s, the source of technology was the Soviet Bloc; in the 1970s, the OECD countries. The first transfer was quite comprehensive, setting the foundation for China's modern industry; the second was highly selective, filling gaps in the development of a few national industries. The transfer modalities varied in the first, e.g., equipment, software, blueprints, training of Chinese technicians, and the presence of Soviet experts; those of the second comprehended a narrower range: principally, equipment and turn-key plants. Thus the first embodied the transfer of expertise, but the second did not: there was no provision for the effective training of Chinese technicians and managers, nor for any substantial presence of foreign experts. The first was financed through government-to-government bilateral agreements, which included countertrade and loans, while the second used cash and deferred payments made directly to the suppliers.

Yet an examination of the effects of both transfers shows two striking similarities: 1) the management of the technology after the transfer, and 2) the extent to which know-how, whether transferred or developed, resulted in innovative capabilities.

In both the major waves of transfer of technology, the suppliers have attempted to influence the Chinese to adapt the management of the enterprise receiving the transfer, if not the management of the technology itself, to the level of sophistication of the transferred technology. The attempts were made quite differently and to widely differing degrees. In the 1950s, the Soviet Union had substantial influence and pressured the Chinese leadership to adopt the Soviet enterprise management system. The thousands of Soviet management experts who went to China as part of the transfer of technology played a key role in the transfer of the Soviet management system to Chinese factories, particularly those new ones that were set up with Soviet aid.

Many factors explained the Soviet Union's behavior. They include its desire to extend its power over a new socialist ally; the orthodoxy of its ways of thinking; and simply the limitation of its knowledge to its own organization and management experience. Also, the Soviets found allies in Chinese leaders who admired their "socialist brother's" political and economic performance, and particularly those leaders who were from China's Northeast, where the Soviet influence was the strongest. Finally, the most important factor in the eyes of both the Soviets and the Chinese was ideological: based on the Marxist materialist view of the primacy of productive forces over relations of production, enterprise organization and management must adapt to the new levels of imported technologies.

The Soviet attempt at introducing its management system was successful principally in China's Northeast, but it did not receive the same degree of support in most enterprises in China. The media began to criticize that alien management system barely two years after supporting its inception. The final blow came with the launching of the Great Leap Forward. All enterprises had to adopt a decentralized organizational structure within a highly decentralized national enterprise management system, in which Communist Party representatives, who often did not possess modern management skills, monopolized the policy and operations decision-making power in enterprises (see chapter 2).

Irrespective of the merits and demerits of the Soviet management system in China, it is interesting to note some of the reasons that China rejected it. The Chinese "love-hate" relation to the introduction of alien ways into China was one reason, with the "hate" side of the equation emphasized from the Great Leap Forward till the start of the post-Mao era.[2] Another reason was the rigidity of the highly structured Soviet system, which emphasized clearly demarcated lines of authority and a high degree of division of labor. Such a "technical" type of organization did not seem to fit with the Chinese emphasis on developing a "human" type of organization preferred by the none-too-technocratically-oriented Chinese Communist Party, which was attempting to consolidate its power over the country. Moreover, the Chinese desired to reduce the growing influence of the Soviets. Finally, China simply did not have the management and technical skills essential to the functioning of a Soviet management system.

During the second major wave of transfer of technology from the West in the 1970s, representatives of supplier companies from the OECD countries shared with their Chinese customers their views as to what organization or management system would be most suitable to the efficient use of the transferred technology. Clearly, unlike the Soviets two decades before, Western businessmen had no influence whatsoever over their customers on this question. In many cases, they were not even aware who the end-user was, nor were they permitted to visit the factory site. Their suggestions often were not relayed beyond the Chinese foreign trade corporation, which, unlike the end-user, might not have had a direct stake in the efficient operation of the imported technology. The infrequent and weak contacts between the Chinese end-users and the Western suppliers prevented the Chinese from properly receiving and considering the suggestions. Even with better communications, it is doubtful whether the suggestions would have had any practical effects. The political situation during the Cultural Revolution, at the time when fierce power struggles coincided with the declining health of Mao Ze-dong, would not have allowed the consideration of management suggestions originating from capitalist countries. Also, China was experiencing yet one more xenophobic period, which precluded the adoption of organization and management suggestions made by outsiders.

The second similarity between the transfers of technology of the 1950s and the 1970s concerns the development of innovative capabilities following the transfer of expertise. In the 1950s, the transfer of expertise was embodied within the transfer of technology from the Soviet Union. It took the form of the massive training of scientists, technicians and managers, and of the presence of large contingents of foreign experts. With its length, breadth, and intensity, the transfer could only have succeeded in imparting technical and managerial know-how to the Chinese. While cut short by the sudden break in Sino-Soviet relations, that transfer of know-how provided China with a large number of skilled people, who, with their compatriots trained abroad prior to Liberation in 1949, formed the core of those who could receive, adapt and use the imported technology, and possibly develop it and make innovations.

Three decades after the beginning of the transfer, an examination of the performance of that contingent, as well as of the technical work force trained in China during that period, reveals a mixed record. The Chinese have been successful in adapting and using Soviet technology, thus contributing to the rapid industrialization of the country. Yet, in general, they have not been in a position to substantially develop it, nor to innovate on it. Visits to Chinese factories in the late 1970s revealed, at best, marginal improvements to production technologies transferred over two decades before. Of course, there are exceptions, such as in the machine-building or military aircraft industries. But even in those cases, China has not come close to international technical standards, nor has it offered major breakthroughs in technical designs.

In the more recent transfers of the 1970s, the Chinese transferred equipment, not know-how, and consequently, no development of innovative capabilities resulted. To remedy the problem, post-Mao Chinese leadership decided to shift its technology transfer policy to emphasize the transfer of know-how over that of equipment, and to allow a substantial foreign role in technical training. The intention of that shift was to develop a domestic ability to innovate on Western technologies already imported or to be imported in the future.[3]

The following is a list of possible reasons, most of which are systemic, for the inability of the Chinese to innovate. Enterprises have been under tremendous pressure to produce according to their yearly quotas in an environment lacking domestic and foreign market competition. Few, if any, tangible incentives were offered for technological innovations, so enterprise management has been unwilling to shoulder the risks associated with innovation. Inadequate resources were allocated by the central government for product development and innovation. A low depreciation rate, and remission of almost all depreciation funds to the State left the enterprise with few financial resources for technological update or innovation. The structure of the research and development establishment was compartmentalized among research institutes belonging to the Academy of Sciences and the industrial ministries, or between regions, or between fields, constraining the type and quality of interaction among technicians and scientists that might have led to innovations. Also, although that structure had allowed the concentration of scarce resources, it had removed those resources from the enterprises, that is, away from the production function, the market, and entrepreneurship, all of which undoubtedly have a positive impact on product innovation and development. In addition, political unrest repeatedly hindered the development of a work environment conducive to research and development. The isolation of China from the international mainstream of scientific and technical information, and the lack of free contact and interaction of Chinese scientists and technicians with their foreign colleagues have obviously been hindering factors. Finally, the general low level of human capital, and the low priority given by the Chinese authorities to developing that capital, could be blamed.

In this chapter, cases of transfer of interrelated technologies will be presented and analyzed. One of the technologies is modern computers. Attention will be given to the process used to select and purchase the equipment, to prepare for its arrival, and to install it. The second type of technology is electronic data processing know-how that allows users to run applications on their computers. The third technology is that of modern management training, the transfer of which is described in detail in the previous chapter. Two separate organizations will be looked at: a university, which acquired the computer equipment as part of its development of a modern management education program; and an industrial enterprise in the process of modernizing its production and management, partly through the purchase of a computer system.

In the study of technology transfer, more attention has usually been given to the supply side. The importance of the recipients' role in the process of the transfer, though intuitively recognized, did not create, until recently, the interest that one would have expected. With the behavior of all the other actors being equal, the recipients' ability to manage properly and efficiently their part of the transfer process is clearly crucial to the outcome of the transfer. Also, their ability to create and manage the necessary environment for the correct and efficient use of the technology once transferred would undoubtedly determine the degree to which the technology is adapted to the local environment, is used according to needs, and is assimilated within the society. The subsequent indigenous development of the technology is a function of the degree of success of both its transfer and use. This chapter will concentrate on the role of the recipients in the management of the transfer process and of the technology itself. The role and action of the recipient government, when relevant, will also be mentioned and analyzed.

The source of data in this chapter is participant observation. In the case of the university, participation spanned the whole process of the transfer, from the identification of the felt need, to the installation of the equipment and the development of the technical expertise. I acted as a transfer facilitator for fifteen months. In the case of the factory, the equipment had been installed for one year already prior to the start of the participant observation. Also, the participation, which covered a period of one year, was limited essentially to that of a consultant on the development of data processing expertise and the use of the imported technology.

Prior to presenting the cases, a brief introduction to the state of the computer industry and the use of computers in China is in order.[4] With the help of the Soviet Union, the Chinese produced their first computers in the late 1950s. Research and development in the computer industry suffered initially from the Sino-Soviet break but picked up in the late 1960s and the 1970s. Computer hardware of the second generation type was being developed and used at the beginning of the 1970s. By the late 1970s, China was able to produce prototypes of third-generation computer hardware, mainly in research institutions and in universities. A major source of computer hardware technology was the few imported computers copied through reverse engineering. Typically, each organization would develop its own prototype and software. Compared with other economically developing countries, and in view of the recent development of the Chinese electronics and computer industries, China's efforts in this field were successful, particularly considering its isolation from the rest of the world.

Yet, upon closer examination, computer research and development and the computer industry in China presented a sorry picture by the end of the 1970s. In research and development, China produced individual pieces of central processing units with medium operating speeds by international standards, but other hardware equipment was entirely neglected. China could only develop outdated, unreliable, slow and low quality input and output peripherals and storage devices.

Also neglected was the development of computer software. Basically, China was unable to provide any software that would have allowed efficient use of its computers. This was another clear indication of China's general favoring of hardware over software and expertise in national technical development. Typically, China's computer users were provided with simple editions of language compilers such as BASIC, ALGOL and FORTRAN. Often, a user would be sold peripherals without the necessary system software to allow him to use them. No computer supplier offered an operating system that would have allowed efficient use of the hardware that China was producing.

In the 1970s the Chinese were proud—rightly so for an economically less developed country—to show foreign visitors some of their most advanced computer installations in universities and research institutes. A closer look at the national computer industry, however, would have given a totally different, and not too positive, impression. The industry was at the stage of a craft industry, with outdated production facilities. Though administratively under the centralized authority of the then Fourth Ministry of Machine-Building, it lacked most of the necessary features to make it into a successful industry. No national standards and norms were set for either the production or specifications of equipment and software. The poor quality of the products, caused by extremely low standards, led to repeated equipment breakdown. The suppliers' after-sale service was basically nonexistent. Computer user groups or active professional associations, which had played a crucial role in facilitating the widespread use of computers in Western countries, did not exist in China.[5]

The users of computers in China in the late 1970s were an elite few. Probably the largest group of users was the military, which had relatively advanced equipment and special software, to achieve technical feats such as the launching of intercontinental ballistic missiles and the launching and recovery of space satellites. The scientific and educational establishment was another large group of users. Both groups used computers principally to solve complicated, mathematically oriented scientific and technical problems. In a sense their computers were used as "number crunchers," which explains the direction of computer research toward higher speed central processing units at the expense of the development of peripherals and system software. Hardly any data processing applications were developed in China to help solve management problems. The lack of reliable data, the neglect of enterprise management, and the lack of the necessary software and equipment—fast input and output and high capacity storage devices—all hindered the use of computers for management purposes, whether in enterprises or in government organizations managing the national economy.[6]

The Transfer of Computer Technology

The Systems Engineering Teachers Training course, mentioned in the previous chapter, was designed to provide introductory instruction in quantitatively oriented management subjects with a heavy emphasis on the use of computers. It was conducted at one of the industrial ministry's universities. Those selected to take the six-month course were mostly university lecturers with a technical background (see chapter 4).

Although most of the subjects in the course curriculum had not been taught in China in any systematic way, if at all, leaders at the ministry and the university

Figure 16.   The Author Meeting the Late Liao Zheng-zhi, Then Vice-Chairman, Standing Committee, National People's Congress, Beijing, 1978.

agreed that a special effort must be made to expose the students to practical applications of course contents. For that course only, 38 students took close to 200 hours of instruction in computer languages, operating systems, and systems design and analysis for a period of six months.[7] For computer instruction, the university authorities combined the classes of that course with those of two other concurrent courses. To respond to the needs of its training program, the university had to provide modern computer facilities adequate to all three of its courses.

In October 1978, the university's computer facilities consisted of two small second-generation computers, both made in China in the 1970s. In addition to weak central processing units, both these computers had limited peripherals and software. Inputting to the system was performed through a slow paper tape and the operator console, and outputting, through a paper tape punch and a slow printer. Neither had any operating system that would have permitted use of the equipment more sophisticated than that of a programmed calculator. The absence of an operating system meant that the computer was dedicated to one user at a time. Both computers had limited internal storage, and only one had a small external storage capability. They were used to teach scientific computer languages, such as ALGOL and FORTRAN, and to help students and faculty solve scientific and engineering problems. It was clear that they could not take the additional load that the systems engineering course would have required. Also, they were inadequate to train students in data processing: they lacked the necessary storage hardware and system software for file management.

The ministry and the university hired me as a foreign expert to help them develop and implement the course. At the earliest stages in the discussion of the course design, I raised the question of the need for computer equipment. My Chinese colleagues assured me that they appreciated this need and would take the necessary steps to procure it. Yet they were not willing to discuss specifics, such as computer brandname, configuration and software.

A few days following my hiring, I was invited to visit the university for a period of ten days and discovered for the first time the total inadequacy of its computer facilities. I was then assured that more suitable computer equipment would be acquired. Nothing more was said. A few days later, I was informed that a DJS-130 computer would be delivered to the university in December, two months prior to the beginning of the course. The computer configuration, that of a small minicomputer, included the central processing unit with a 32K internal memory, a slow teletype operator console, a cathode-ray tube (CRT) terminal, a printer, a paper tape reader and punch, and a plotter. Apart from a BASIC interpreter, no other software would be provided by the manufacturer. It was clear that this configuration would not fit the requirements of the course.

To purchase domestically a sophisticated piece of equipment, such as a computer system, a Chinese organization must obtain both permission and the necessary allocation of funds from its superior organization. The buyer—the end-user and representatives of its superior organization—and the seller negotiate the equipment allocation to the prospective buyer, its specifications, and the terms of its purchase and delivery. Since the production and sale of electronic computers comes under the yearly economic plan in China, and they are in short supply, the time lag between the end user's request and the delivery of the equipment is measured in months, if not in years.

Yet the university obtained its DJS-130 in a short time. Both ministry and university representatives cooperated closely to expedite the order. Through personal connections, including an electronic engineer working in the computer factory, the ministry and the university were able to convince the plant to have one of its systems delivered to the university rather than to the original customer.

Representatives of the university suspected that the configuration of the computer system would not satisfy the minimum computer specifications needed for the course. They also knew prior to the purchase that computer equipment manufactured in that plant was inferior to that manufactured in other electronics plants in China. They were aware that the manufacturer would supply a BASIC interpreter but no operating system or other system software that would allow linking the central processing unit to much of the peripheral equipment purchased, including the CRT

Figure 17.   The Author with Members of the Payroll Project Team, Shanghai, 1979.

terminal, plotter, and printer. Yet they were satisfied with their coup: the purchase and delivery of a whole computer system hardware in less than three months.

Clearly they felt that an incremental approach to obtaining the needed equipment was optimum: first, get a basic system from wherever possible, whatever its quality, configuration and software support; then work step by step to bring the system as close as possible to the desired specifications. They felt that they did not want to go through the standard procedure to purchase a Chinese system to avoid the waiting period of at least one year. Anyway, the system would not satisfy many of the required specifications, since China was not in a position domestically to supply disk drives for external storage capability, nor the software to support many of the peripherals, let alone a time-sharing or multi-user environment.

The alternative to importing a whole minicomputer system was not satisfactory, at least in the short term, for two reasons: the ministry might not have been able to secure the relatively large sum in foreign exchange for a small project such as this course, assuming it was willing to support such an alternative. Also, the system would not have been delivered to the university for a year or more, due to the lengthy import procedures.[8] So to the ministry and the university, there was simply no feasible alternative to the one they had followed.

To bring the DJS-130 up to the desired specifications, the Chinese decided to send me to North America to purchase compatible software and hardware, including terminals, disk drives, an operating system with a time-sharing capability, and language compilers. It was expected that the purchased equipment and software would arrive in China in a little over two months, in time for the beginning of the course, in February.[9] Representatives of the ministry initiated complex and time-consuming negotiations with many foreign-trade-related organizations—including the Ministry of Finance, the Bank of China, and a foreign trade corporation—to obtain permission to make the purchases, to assess the total cost of the purchases, and to obtain the needed foreign exchange. Also, special permission had to be granted to have the purchase made by an individual—who also happened to be a non-Chinese—and not by the foreign trade corporation. All this was done within four weeks, a record time, thanks to strong support, which came from as high a level as the State Council.

The DJS-130 computer was a version of a Data General minicomputer that the Chinese had copied using reverse engineering techniques. The engineer from the electronics plant, who had helped the university obtain the computer in such a short time, acted as the technical advisor for hardware, and I acted as the advisor for software. The engineer was confident that the peripherals to be imported could be attached to the main frame with little effort in terms of time and manpower. In his view, it would take only a few days after the equipment delivery to design and build the necessary hardware interfaces and have the entire system operational. I was less optimistic. Though not fully aware of the technical abilities present at the plant, I felt that inexperience in working with the equipment to be imported, possibly incomplete technical specification of that equipment, as well as management-related delays at the plant level, would cause a far later delivery date than the one promised by the engineer. I also pointed out that, even if the interfaces were operational within a short time, adapting the imported software to support the operations of the system would be complex and time-consuming. Representatives of the university seemed to lean towards the engineer's definition of system operationality as being hardware compatibility, with little regard to software. They made the necessary arrangements with the electronics plant to manufacture the interfaces for the imported equipment, once it was delivered to the university.

On arriving in North America, I quickly identified feasible equipment and potential sellers. However, I soon became aware of the revolutionary development of the microcomputer industry. It was clear that with the amount of funds needed to purchase the peripherals to attach to the DJS-130, entire ready-to-use microcomputer hardware and software systems could be acquired, providing the university with far more advanced computing technology and power, a wider range of systems and application software, and a far superior capability for a multi-user environment than the original plan would have allowed. Also, in buying entire computer systems rather than peripherals, the university would benefit from the computer supplier's technical and marketing support.

Notwithstanding the deadline I was working under, I thought it would be beneficial in the long run for my Chinese employer to consider the new alternative prior to making the purchases. I dropped the original plan; instead, I studied the microcomputer industry, contacted a number of potential suppliers, and had many systems demonstrated to me. In sum, I collected all the technical and commercial data relevant to making the final selection of computer equipment. Upon my return to China, I presented the two sets of alternatives and the data I had collected to my colleagues at the ministry and the university.

My Chinese colleagues were receptive to the new alternative since it was clear to them that microcomputers presented definite advantages. They and the engineer questioned me in some detail on the technical performance of the new computers and on the rapidly developing microcomputer market. To facilitate the decision-making process, I drew sample configurations and cost estimates for all feasible computers for them and the engineer to study. The leaders of the university quickly obtained permission from the ministry to switch the purchases to microcomputers.

The choice of suppliers was narrowed to two. Both offered similar hardware, basic software support and terms of delivery. There was no substantial price difference between them. The first supplier had two models of hard disk drives ready for delivery. The second had announced new state-of-the-art hard disk drives for delivery within the year, and provided software to support a multi-user environment. Moreover, its top executives had indicated to me in the United States their strong interest in entering the China market.

Representatives of the University and the engineer concluded that they would prefer the first supplier, because it had hard disk drives readily available and deferred to me to select the final configuration. I advsised my Chinese colleagues to reconsider their choice of supplier, arguing that a multi-user computer environment was important for the course and that the immediate availability of hard disk drives was less important, since the configuration included floppy disk drives, and the benefits of post-sale marketing and service support that the second supplier would probably provide would be significant considering its strong interest in the China market. Also, I indicated that the second manufacturer enjoyed a more solid reputation in this young, still risky industry. To clarify the significance of post-sale support, basically non-existent in China, I explained the nature of the customer-supplier relationship in Western capitalist countries, and the philosophy and attitudes that underlie that relationship, contrasting them to those prevalent in China.

Although they had the data that formed the basis of my arguments, it was clear that the Chinese had not considered these factors, yet quickly realized their importance. After short consultations among themselves and the engineer, the representatives of the university decided to reverse their earlier decision and select the second supplier. They agreed to my suggestion of signing a purchase contract with an agent, since the supplier had little experience in exporting its products aboard, let alone to China. The agent, who had a 10-year experience in the China market, would be in a better position to expedite the delivery of the goods and to provide satisfactory communication among all concerned parties, thanks to her frequent China visits. The ministry and the university asked me to enter into negotiation with the agent and to sign the purchase contract once an agreement was reached.

A total of four microcomputer systems, each with floppy disk drives and printers and system and application software packages, were purchased. Two systems supported a multi-user environment of up to seven users each. Thus, simultaneous access of up to sixteen users was possible. At the manufacturer's recommendation, a selection of spare parts and accessories, such as printer ribbons and floppy disks, was included in the contract. Under a special rubric, and at the request of the university, a few thousand dollars were transferred to the agent in the United States for the purchase of yet unspecified spare parts and accessories for future maintenance. This was done to avoid having to go once more through the cumbersome procedures of obtaining foreign exchange, or the risk of a denial of foreign exchange.[10]

When the equipment was ready for shipment, delays in the opening of the letter of credit were encountered. One month later I was indirectly informed of the cause of the delays. Both the Bank of China and the foreign trade corporation refused to authorize the opening of the letter of credit on the basis that I had the authority to sign the contract outside but not inside China. Following negotiations, the ministry reached an agreement with the bank, but not with the foreign trade corporation, which felt that its legal prerogatives were not being respected.[11] Finally, to preserve a good working relationship with the corporation, the ministry acceded to the latter's demands. The corporation and the agent signed a new contract with terms identical to the original one, which was cancelled. This incident delayed the delivery of the computers by over three months. They were installed and became partially operational only in the last two weeks of the six-month-long course.

Soon after the signing of the original contract, the university began to plan the installation of the computer equipment. It decided to remodel an existing facility with ample room for expansion. The ministry provided the university with a generous budget comparable in size to the purchase price of the computer equipment. Thanks to the ministry's support and to strong industry connections, the university was able to cut down substantially on the delays normally required to get an allocation from outside the plan of the needed manpower, materials and auxilliary equipment to set up the computer center. Still, obtaining the allocation and ensuring the delivery of the materials and equipment was time-consuming, requiring lengthy negotiations with local government and enterprise representatives. For example, to ensure the delivery of the environment control equipment to the university and not to another competing customer, the computer center director-designate had to be physically present at the manufacturing plant during the days of the expected shipping date.

The actual remodeling of the facility began about two months later than originally planned, leaving very little time to meet the deadline. Yet the university leadership felt confident that the work would be finished in time and would not delay the installation of the equipment.

The university leadership appointed a director of the new Systems Engineering Computer Center, as the new installation would be known. He was a member of the faculty in the department of automation and systems engineering, with a background in automation, some experience in the use of the university's Chinese-made computers, but no working knowledge of English. Three of his immediate tasks were to design the physical layout of the installation; to coordinate the installation of the equipment and training of the center personnel; and to set up the proper procedures to govern the use of the computer facilities by the faculty and students.

In addition to the new center director, the university leadership selected eight people to become the center's technical personnel, and three younger people to become the clerical support personnel of the center.[12] Apart from two more senior people, the technical personnel were recent graduates of the university, who were assigned by the State to remain there as junior faculty.[13] The personnel was divided into two groups: the first was to install the equipment and solve hardware-related problems; the second was to install the software. Both groups were headed by one of the more senior members of the center's personnel. A division of labor was set up in each of these two groups. The electronics engineer advised the first group, while I advised the second and the center director on the overall installation schedule and coordination.

As in the case of the remodeling of the location, the center personnel faced a close deadline in preparing for the layout and installation of the equipment. Yet for weeks, it seemed that no detailed planning was undertaken by the center director. An equipment layout plan and an installation plan were finally presented by the center director after I repeatedly reminded the university leadership of the delay and pressed for action.

The little experience in computer science that the technical personnel had, for those who had any, was limited to the use of the university's second-generation computers, that is, to writing and executing programs in ALGOL or FORTRAN. Some had rudimentary training in BASIC, while others, particularly the senior members of the team, had electrical or electronic engineering, or automation and process control backgrounds. Only a few of them could read English comfortably enough to make adequate use of the technical materials supplied by the computer manufacturer. In view of the technical training and language handicaps that the team was facing, it was decided that one or two persons would concentrate their efforts on learning one aspect of the computer hardware or software, with the proviso that the self-acquired knowledge would be shared with the rest of the team through presentations and discussions. Also, the decision was made to translate key manuals into Chinese. Both the electronics engineer and I were resources that members of the team could call on.

Neither of the original two deadlines—to have the computer center ready to receive the computers and to have the teams ready to install the computer hardware and software—were met. Yet the effect of missing the deadlines was minimal, since the shipment of the computer to China was delayed, as mentioned above. The construction team turned the computer center over to the university only a week prior to the arrival of the computer. Also, the installation team used the two-month delay in the shipment to catch up on its own preparations.

The cheerful feeling of expectation that the Chinese at the university had sustained despite difficulties reached a new height when the computer equipment arrived on campus. As planned, the hardware installation team soon began its work, installing and testing the systems one by one. Overall, the hardware installation went smoothly, partly because the microcomputers were designed for easy installation. The minor difficulties encountered were caused by equipment or parts damaged during shipping, which were interchanged with undamaged ones, or by members of the team not following the installation instructions written in English. The latter problem was gradually eliminated as the team's experience increased.

The first computer was installed about three weeks before the scheduled end of the course. So that they would have the opportunity to use the computers, the students were given access to a computer as soon as it was operational. Yet their use of the equipment was rather rudimentary, since neither the faculty nor the computer center personnel had time to develop teaching materials for more advanced use of the facilities.

With the installation of the first microcomputer, the importance of the management of the computer center became evident. The center director devised a schedule and a set of rules, approved by his superior, for both faculty and students for using the computer facilities. The center was open six days a week for one shift of eight hours a day, including the one to two hours of rest customary in China. Time slots were allocated to the class of the Systems Engineering Teachers Course, and a tight time limit was set for each user.

The Transfer of Data Processing Expertise

The Case of the University

The previous chapter briefly described the applied computer science instruction component of the Systems Engineering Teachers Training course. The principal purpose of that component was to introduce the students to the use of computers in the management of Chinese enterprises. The instruction spanned a wide range of courses, all of which were relevant to the potential management user, including system software, computer language programming, and systems design and analysis.

The course did not achieve one of its original objectives: transferring applied computer expertise. Such expertise included the ability to write computer programs, to assess computer configurations needed for certain management applications, and to recognize the basic technical and managerial concepts and steps to the design, development and implementation of electronic data processing applications.

To remedy the problem, at the end of the systems engineering course, scheduled for July 1978, representatives of the university requested, at my suggestion, that the ministry allow a selection of the best students to remain at the university for practical training in computer data processing by me. Since the students were expected to disseminate their knowledge of data processing within their respective universities, such practical training would definitely help their work in the future. Also, the university recommended that a smaller size class be selected to avoid the problems caused by the 100-student computer science class of the Systems Engineering Teachers Training Course, and to allow better practical training. Moreover, holding the training class would make efficient use of my remaining six months of employment with the university.

Following the ministry's approval, 12 of the best students were selected to take part in the training course, which was composed of two parts.[14] The first and shorter part was the study and analysis of a computerized production planning and control package marketed by a major United States computer firm. This exercise complemented the short introductory course on data processing systems design and analysis offered in the Systems Engineering Teacher Training Course and introduced the students to the structure of a computerized system, its tasks and performance, and the data flow within it. The study of the package was conducted in the form of a workshop, in which the students played the major role in analyzing, presenting and discussing the materials and I acted as an advisor and monitor to the class. The second, more substantial part of the course was the undertaking of a data processing project. To be selected, projects had to address actual problems faced by operating organizations; be undertaken with an adequate level of support from the hosting organization; be of a managerial nature and susceptible to systems engineering and electronic data processing solutions; present no major technical or managerial complication; and be of a manageable size, to allow the students the time to be involved in all facets of the project.

Three projects were selected. One was an inventory control system for a machine-building factory considered among the better managed factories in Shanghai, and whose leadership was cooperative and eager to modernize its management. Yet the factory had no historical data useful to the design of the project, and thus it was difficult to determine the parameters of the inventory control system.[15] With those constraints, the project was limited to a general analysis of the factory's inventory control system, the design of an algorithm to help improve it and the development of a computer program using that algorithm. Without the availability of data the program could not be tested.

Figure 18.   Modernization Knocks at the Door—Promoting "Full and Efficient
Business Propaganda," Shanghai, 1979.
(Photograph by Author)

One student, a faculty member of the university, was assigned to that project and developed the program using the university computer facilities, since the factory had no computer of its own. In view of the factory's poor environment for computerization of its management, the usefulness of the project was questionable.

The second project was to help another machine-building factory to develop a preliminary production planning and control system, which would serve as the basic design and foundation for a more detailed system. Details on the university-factory cooperation and on the selection and development of the project are provided in the section of this chapter titled "The Case of the Factory."

Eight students, or the majority of the class, were assigned to the third project, which was to create a computerized payroll system for the 1,400 staff members of the university. The project was small to medium size and presented no technical or managerial complication. Also, the university authorities cooperated enthusiastically with the students on this project. The payroll system was developed using the computer installation at the university. The rest of this section details the conduct of this project and its results.

In view of the educational and professional level of the students—all were college graduates and most were college instructors—and the practical nature of the training, I decided to turn the class into a workshop and to conduct the work in a manner similar to a real data processing project. The class acted as the project team, and I became its project leader and technical advisor. No classroom instruction was scheduled. Only when the students or I needed to clarify a technical concept or aspect of the project was a lecture conducted. As in a real-life project, the team established a plan of action and a schedule, defining the various stages and substages of the project. Individual responsibilities within the team were assigned as each stage was implemented.

The students took part in the following activities of the project:

—conducting interviews with, and collecting data from, the user;
—studying the project's technical feasibility and overall design options;
—presenting the results of the above two tasks to the payroll department and to the top leadership of the university, who were then asked to select one from among the design options that the team had offered;
—collecting additional data and designing the system in detail;
—for each of the subsystems, designing, developing and testing the programs and the data files;
—testing each subsystem and the overall system;
—establishing operating procedures for the user; and
—running parallel operations.

The attempt to have the students operate in as close to a real environment as possible succeeded. The objective of this approach was to train them not only in the techniques of data processing but also in the management of data processing projects, since the students would be teaching in higher education institutions in programs similar to those of operations management and industrial engineering in the West.

The result of the class project was a data-base computerized payroll application for the whole university staff, probably the most advanced in design in China at the time. The design of its data base would allow the expansion of the system to include other applications useful to the management of the university. In addition to the normal computation of salary and remuneration for a member of the staff, the application presented 15 other features particular to the university.[16] A major benefit introduced by the application was the establishment, for the first time, of a university-wide codified identification system for the staff, which could be used for other administrative and academic applications.

The system provided the user with a reduction of computing and updating data anywhere from tenfold to close to one thousand-fold, depending on which aspect of the application was considered. Despite the limited physical capabilities of the microcomputer peripherals, the payroll system, if implemented, would have reduced the personnel need by a factor of 12. In addition to the monthly payroll slips for the 1,400 staff members, the system produced up-to-date payroll files, executive and control reports, and other administrative reports useful to the payroll department. Yet, for reasons discussed in the next chapter, the payroll department did not adopt the application, which the project team ran successfully in parallel for three months.

The project team was composed of five lecturers, whose ages ranged approximately from early thirties to mid-forties, two junior instructors in their twenties, one engineer and a payroll department liaison person also in her twenties. The older group in the team was more capable intellectually and technically, and had, in addition to more professional experience, more serious academic training, prior to the Cultural Revolution. On the technical level, none of the members of the team had any experience in data processing systems design and analysis, and their level of writing computer programs was generally low, though uneven. As mentioned earlier in the chapter, they had just finished attending close to 200 hours of computer science classroom instruction, with basically no benefit whatsoever from practical training. Apart from two members, all the students could read and comprehend English, so they had access to the computer technical data provided by the U.S. manufacturer.

Supplementary training was provided to familiarize the students with the use of the computer equipment, help them write simple programs, and introduce them to the concepts of data files and data base management. The students then worked as a group, with little division of labor, on the collection and analysis of data, on the formulation of the various general design options, on the presentation that was made to the executive of the university, and on the overall systems design as finally selected (see the list of project activities above). With the beginning of the development of the first subsystem, a division of labor was introduced, based on the requirement of the design of the subsystem. Each student, or couple of students, was responsible for developing and testing the assigned programs. The team members' work was coordinated through individual communication and scheduled project team meetings.

In the first six weeks of the project, my role was crucial. I acted as the team's technical and managerial leader, training the team members to a reasonable technical competence. I closely guided the students in their work in the first stages of the project, up to and including the design of the first subsystem of the application. Whenever needed, I acted as a technical advisor to individual members of the team. By the end of that period, it became clear that the project team could carry much more responsibility for the development and implementation of the application because the completed basic design of the overall system had laid the foundation for the detailed design of each of its subsystems and because most team members had learned quickly.

The management of the project was turned over to two members of the team. Members of the team resolved most of the technical problems among themselves. Those with more advanced technical knowledge formulated the detailed design of the remaining subsystems. The team kept the work pattern previously set: a combination of a division of labor, with regular coordination and integration sessions. I acted only as a technical and managerial advisor to the team, meeting with them for one-half to one day a week to respond to unresolved technical questions, monitor work progress, and discuss the planning of subsequent stages of the project.

At the end of the fourth month, I left China. Within a period of five months from the actual beginning of the project, the application was developed, the subsystems were tested individually, and preparations were being made to test the application in its entirety and to commence the parallel operation. At that point, the team disbanded, each member returning to his respective work place. The two junior members of the team, who were from the university, successfully performed the final test and ran the payroll system in parallel for three consecutive months.

The Case of the Factory

In this section a case of the introduction of data processing in a Chinese factory, one year after the delivery and installation of imported computer equipment, is examined.[17] Although it will not treat questions related to the selection, purchase and installation of the equipment, the case will point to many of their effects on the efficient use of the transferred technology.

The factory belonged to the same ministry that sponsored the Systems Engineering Teacher Training Course. It was established in the 1950s, with the help of the Soviet Union, to produce large industrial machinery. In its production capacity and product quality, it ranked among the top five plants in China. The ministry's jurisdiction over it was shared with the authorities of the province in which the plant was located, a normal situation in China's State industrial organization system.

The factory did not possess the necessary internal resources to undertake major technological innovations and improvements, nor to design new products or product lines. Like most other industrial plants in China, it could only make minor technological improvements to the design of its products or to its production processes. The ministry was the plant's main source of domestically developed technology and of foreign exchange for the acquisition and adoption of foreign technologies. In the early 1970s, the plant's product technology, though of the most advanced type then existing in China, clearly trailed behind that of its average Western counterpart. Its products were expensive to produce, bulky and heavy, and energy inefficient.

As indicated in the first part of this chapter, in the early and mid-1970s China purchased a substantial amount of modern technologies in a number of industrial sectors, particularly fertilizer, chemical, petrochemical, and machine-building. The transfer of technology from the West and Japan took the form of turn-key plants, large purchases of equipment, and, in exceptional cases, licensing. As part of this wave of technology transfer, the ministry decided to have the plant update the design of its product line and its production technology. Millions of United States dollars were spent on advanced product designs and production technologies, a complete computer system imported from West Germany, and a number of large machines imported from West Europe and Japan to set up new production facilities. These transferred technologies were expected to expand the plant's production capacity, improve product quality and replace the 1950s-vintage Soviet technologies used at the plant since its establishment two decades earlier.

The terms of the purchase of the machinery included the provision by the suppliers of technical teams to install the machinery in the factory and to provide initial guidance for their operation, but no further provision for technical or managerial training. As part of the purchase agreement for the new product designs, the supplier trained a small team of Chinese technicians and engineers in West Germany for a short period of time. As for the computer purchase contract, there was no provision for personnel training whatsoever, the Chinese being content to receive the technical manuals usually provided to customers along with the computer equipment.

The imported computer system was a medium- to large-size minicomputer, with an adequate size internal memory, a selection of input and output devices and system software packages, including a time-sharing capability. As part of the modernization plans for the plant, the computer was to introduce electronic data processing into the factory to improve its production management with the aid of applications such as planning and control, inventory management and control, and workshop production management. The plant wanted to build a computerized data base to be shared by all the applications it intended to develop. The Chinese selected the same computer system that their West German licensor used for the management of its own production. The licensor offered to sell the Chinese the application software needed to run the computer, including the data base structure crucial to the implementation of the data processing applications. The Chinese decided not to purchase the software, claiming that their plant operations differed from those of the West German supplier. They preferred to develop the entire software themselves, tailoring it to their specific needs. No doubt they were also unwilling to make additional foreign exchange expenditures to purchase the software.

After the computer equipment was installed, a computer team was formed to develop data processing applications. The team was headed by a director of the computer center, who also acted as the director of systems and data processing for the factory. Among the team members, only one man seemed to play the role of the systems analyst. The team included a few operators and programmers. Contrary to what would be expected, neither the director nor the systems analyst had had adequate technical training, either formal or informal, in their respective areas of responsibility. Since no one in the factory had received any training in the operation and use of the imported equipment nor in the design of data processing systems from the computer manufacturer or from any other source, the computer center's first priority was to train its own personnel.

A year after the installation of the computer, the computer center was in a sorry state. Not one single application had been developed, let alone implemented. No viable strategy for developing and introducing data processing applications in the factory had yet been formulated. Should the factory develop a production planning and control system, an inventory management and control system, a payroll

Figure 19.   The Author Meeting Bo Yi-bo, Then Vice-Premier, Beijing, 1979.

system, or a plant data base similar to the one used by the West German supplier and about which the Chinese had sketchy knowledge? On an experimental basis, the systems analyst was compiling a file that included characteristics and specifications of parts and components, as a first step for the possible establishment of a plant data base. The computer center director leaned more toward developing an inventory control system. All the programmers were still learning, on their own, how to write programs in COBOL and FORTRAN languages. The operators seemed to feel confident about operating the computer equipment but had no application to run on it.

The ministry was clearly displeased with the factory's lack of progress in applying the computer to the management of its production. At the end of that first year, the ministry ordered that the factory develop at least one data processing application within the following 12 months. At the same time, the leadership of the ministry suggested that the factory management might invite members of the Systems Engineering Teachers Training class to help it develop the use of its computer, and initiated the first contacts between the factory and the university.

The university leadership was initially eager for its systems engineering students to take part in projects at the factory. Soon, however, it became clear that the factory management doubted the usefulness of the students, at a time when it was under serious pressure from the ministry to perform. Finally, it agreed to cooperate with the university and suggested that the students write programs for the applications that the factory—mainly in the person of the computer center director—was about to decide on. At that stage of negotiation, the plant was considering the simultaneous development of computerized production planning and control, inventory management and control, data base system, and possibly payroll system. The overall time-frame the factory had for writing the programs for all these applications was one year—the deadline set by the ministry.

The university representatives felt that it was impossible to commit the students, most of whom were faculty members, to the role of mere programmers and for long enough to develop the applications that the factory intended to develop. In their view, the project should be small, to allow the students to be involved in all its stages and to finish it within a short period of time, and it should not present any technical or managerial complications. The university also wished to retain a certain degree of autonomy in the conduct of the project to ensure that its development fitted with these criteria. Finally, it was clear to the university representatives that the factory's proposal was not feasible. It grossly underestimated the work that the simultaneous undertaking of the applications would entail; and it suffered from the absence of feasibility studies, design analysis, technically qualified personnel, and the involvement of the factory management.

The negotiations were deadlocked so the university obtained permission from the ministry to have me take part in them. To introduce me to the situation at the factory, the first day of the first round of negotiations was used for presentations on the factory's operations and plans for modernization, and for site visits, including the computer center and the newly arrived machinery from Europe and Japan. Once the negotiations actually resumed, it became clear that both parties wanted to get my opinion on the factory's plans for the development of its data processing applications.

Representatives of the factory, principally one of its deputy-directors, the computer center director and the systems analyst, made the presentations. In my mind, the university's views were confirmed: the factory personnel were clearly under pressure to develop a computerized application, yet they lacked direction and both the knowledge and experience to do so. It was also clear that the factory's top executives considered the development and introduction of those applications to be technical, lying within the responsibilities of the computer center, rather than managerial, requiring top leadership's close involvement.

During that round of negotiations, the deputy-director and some of his colleagues began to realize that their original plans might not be entirely feasible. Subsequent meetings with the leadership of the factory provided the leadership with the basic managerial and technical concepts relevant to introducing the use of a computer in the management of the factory. Discussions were held on questions of project selection, necessary resources for the development of projects, the plant management and the computer center personnel's respective roles in the implementation of the project, and the impact of introducing the contemplated applications on the management and production of the factory. Finally, the factory's deputy-director invited members of the university faculty and me to give formal presentations on systems engineering and data processing to the executive of the factory and to its computer personnel. That invitation marked a turning point in the factory-university relationship.

The university seemed to have had three principal objectives for bringing me into the negotiations. The first was to make the factory management realize that its plan for developing the data processing applications was not feasible. The university hoped that I—as a systems engineer and a foreigner—would give its position more credibility in the eyes of the factory leadership. The second objective was to give the factory leadership the opportunity to learn about the use of computers in the management of the factory. The last objective was to affect the negotiations positively so that the university could collaborate with the factory.

Indeed, a verbal agreement was finally reached between the university and the factory and received the approval of the ministry. The decision was to develop a general production planning and control application, using operations research techniques. It was designed to lead to a more detailed computerized planning and control system in the future and to be compatible with the development of other production-related applications, such as inventory management and control. The project had two co-leaders, one from each institution. The project team included the students, members of the computer personnel, and representatives of the user department within the factory. The management of the factory agreed to provide the project team with the necessary support, such as data from the users, the management's own participation in the decision-making when needed, and material resources. As part of a compromise reached between the two institutions, the university acquiesced in having two of its students take part in the development of an inventory control system, a project that the computer center director at the factory still wanted to undertake.

Following initial minor problems, remedied thanks to pressures exerted by the ministry and the goodwill of representatives of the university and the factory, the project progressed rapidly. A few months after the start of the project, the team finished its work, the high quality of which was recognized by all concerned parties. The inventory control project was facing serious difficulties at the time. The factory leadership suggested that the factory and the university enter into a formal long-term agreement, in which the systems engineering students would regularly take part in the development of production management data processing packages at the factory in the future.

Postscript

As part of her modernization, China has been experiencing another wave of transfer of technology expected to last for many years to come. The types and sources of

Figure 20.   Early Privately-Run Business, Guilin, 1978.
(Photograph by Author)

the transferred technologies are varied, touching virtually every economic sector and originating mainly from OECD countries. As in the 1950s, the Chinese have adopted the whole gamut of transfer modes, including turn-key projects, licensing, consulting, equipment and, new to socialist China, joint equity ventures.

It is too early to assess China's performance in management of the transfer and to do so requires an extensive study beyond the scope of this postscript. Yet it is worth commenting on the effects of recent shifts in systemic factors on the efficiency of the transfer, based on preliminary impressionistic observations.

The broadening of foreign trade and the increasing decentralization of the foreign trade system have allowed far closer contacts of end-users with foreign suppliers and with the international markets. The range of technologies, suppliers and transfer modes available to end-users has widened substantially. This is also due to a radical ideological shift away from the narrowly-defined self-reliance policy and from equating technology with hardware exclusively. Currently Chinese transfer recipients are in a position to purchase training and consulting services and other forms of know-how, and have begun to truly appreciate the importance of the hardware/software package for a successful technology transfer.

On the negative side, China's weak investment analysis methods and account-ability system, her highly imperfect market mechanisms, the remnant effects of her past isolation and inexperience in the management of the transfer of technology and international markets are still adversely affecting efficient transfers of technology. Despite the last few years' serious efforts at developing managerial and technical human resources, the high rates of transfer of technology and of economic growth have caused the supply of such resources to lag far behind the demand. This shortage of skills has been a major factor in the underutilization of transferred technologies.[18]

Notwithstanding noteworthy successes and recent positive trends, systemic factors lagging behind seemingly correct policies have still plagued the efficient implementation of such policies; the technology transfer policy is but one example. The characteristically slow process for changing such systemic factors, combined with pressures exercised by a rapid economic growth, allows only a slow resolution of these problems.

6

Analysis

In the last two chapters, the cases of the management of the transfer of three inter-related technologies were presented. They were modern management techniques, computers, and electronic data processing. In the first case, detailed in chapter 4, one industrial ministry attempted to design, set up and implement a management training program for 38 educators working in higher education institutions under the ministry. The training program focused principally on the use of quantitative methods and systems approach to solving managerial problems, hence its name "Systems Engineering Teachers Training Course." Also, early attempts at reviving the field of management nationally and the importance of the foreign factor in those efforts were described. The second case, discussed in chapter 5, detailed the transfer of computer technology to the university where the course was taking place. The establishment of the need for the technology, the selection of the equipment, its purchase, the preparation for its arrival, and its management were presented. Finally, the third technology was computer know-how in the form of electronic data processing. Two cases were presented: the university's, where the management training program was taking place; and the factory's, where a computer system had been acquired from the West as part of a comprehensive program to update the factory's product line and modernize its management.

In all cases, special attention was given to the process of the transfer and to the management of that process. The latter included the diagnosis of the problem, the concept of its technical and managerial solution, the search and selection of the technology, the managerial, technical and material preparations to receive it, and the early use of that technology. Also emphasized was the management of the technology, once it was received, with a description of the level and quality of its use by the recipient.

Five types of factors seem to shed light on the management of both the process and the technology itself. They are: 1) ideological values and economic concepts, 2) systemic factors, 3) human resources, 4) the type of technology, and 5) the presence of foreign consultants.

Ideological Values and Economic Concepts

Ideological Values

In this section we will discuss the ideological values that have crucially influenced transfer of technology decisions or the decision-making process in China.

Views on hardware and software.   Chinese interpretation of Marxist materialist economic philosophy puts great, perhaps undue, stress on the importance of hardware technology (production forces). Knowledge, scientific as well as technical, is considered an outcome of man's materialistic experience, and thus is subordinate. This view clearly disregards the growing importance of know-how and practical knowledge, including software, be it managerial or technical, in our post-industrial society. In a sense Marxist philosophy, developed in the mid-nineteenth century at the beginning of the Industrial Revolution, or its interpretation, has not been updated by its followers in China to reflect fundamental changes in the technological structure of the world. One hundred years ago, terms such as hardware, software, know-how did not exist. Their present currency reflects an undeniable evolution in society's technology and technological concepts.

Yet, as one result of the Chinese interpretation of Marxist materialist views, the management of enterprises has been grossly neglected, whereas the production capacity has greatly expanded. Equipment or plants have been imported with little regard to the transfer or the development of technical or managerial skills, and to the software. Computerization is mistakenly identified with the mere acquisition of computer hardware. Developing software is often mistakenly interpreted as the writing of a few programs, underestimating the skills and time involved and the complexity of the tasks. Lack of experience and the emphasis on hardware is reflected in the comment often made to me: "Once the computer [i.e., the equipment] arrives, our management problems will be solved!"

The concept of self-reliance.   This notion, strengthened by the Sino-Soviet Rift, is valuable only if basic core of managerial and technical skills and know-how are present. Otherwise the self-reliance notion is not only unproductive (does not get the job done), but also counter-productive (waste of scarce resources, dampening psychological effects, shoddy standards, etc.). This is shown in the case of the data processing in the factory. Thus, the usefulness of self-reliance in and of itself may be questionable. It has rather to be assessed within the environment in which it is applied.

Economic Concepts

In our analysis of economic and managerial questions, we often use standards, criteria, and measurements familiar to the society and the culture we live in. Basic economic concepts are usually at the source of all those standards, criteria and measurements, the common use of which often makes us take for granted the fundamental role that those concepts have played in shaping our critical faculties and our world outlook. In this section, the absence or the weak presence in China of some Western economic concepts will be discussed, and its consequences to the management of the transfer process and of the technologies pointed out.

The concept of opportunity cost.   This basic economic concept existing in capitalist economies was not part of the enterprise economic decision-making process in China. Opportunity cost implies the presence of a reasonable degree of freedom in selecting any one of the available opportunities based on established selection criteria and access to the resources, though finite, needed to truly exercise a choice. In a sense, opportunity cost requires that the enterprise operate in an economy that possesses substantial market elements. In 1978, ''opportunity cost'' did not exist in the Chinese language.

In the 1970s, when showing installed imported equipment to visitors, enterprise representatives proudly stated that the machinery was operated self-reliantly, that is with no training provided by the foreign supplier. What was the opportunity cost of that self-reliance, i.e., which of the alternatives—presence or absence of foreign training—was economically beneficial to the enterprise or the society as a whole? Also, opportunity cost was not a part of either the university's or the factory's decision-making process when they purchased the DJS-130 and the West German computers, respectively.

The concept of marginal analysis.   A typical approach to cost or revenue analysis in China is an average analysis, rather than a marginal analysis. Often, average cost is reduced by cutting down on the purchase of software and training services, neither of which is tangible in the materialist ideological view commonly held in China. Yet the marginal return of software and training is usually very high. Their presence or absence determines whether the technology transfer recipient will be able to use the technology effectively, as the case of the factory has shown.

The concept of the return on investment.   Although the concept of return on investment exists in China, it is very weak both conceptually and operationally. Other factors, such as political considerations, economic objectives, and cultural-ideological values, play a far more important part in the allocation of resources. If and when this concept is used, its measurements are usually partial and simplistic, principally the payback period. Moreover, China's appropriation system makes capital appear to be a free good to the enterprise, making any investment analysis deficient. Had the return on investment been part of performance evaluation, the computer purchase decisions in the case studies would probably have been different.

Systemic Factors

For our purpose, systemic factors are divided into the general economic system and the foreign trade system. Although the latter is part of the former, it is examined separately because of its importance to the transfer of technology.

The Economic System

Scarcity. Facing an economy characterized by scarcity of resources and highly centralized, taut planning, the management of an enterprise dreads supply shortages, which in the case of China cannot be remedied through market mechanisms and mean high costs and the non-fulfillment of State quotas. The usual way to avoid them is to hoard scarce input, since the cost of hoarding is well below that of shortage. Also, facing a sellers' market, the management adopts a satisficing attitude to whatever production input it can get hold of. In our case, this is illustrated by the ministry and the university being content with, in fact proud of, their acquisition of the DJS-130 computer equipment, however inadequate for the needs of the management education program. Their strategy was to accept whatever was available and gradually bring the computer facility up to the desired state—probably an optimum approach in view of the scarce computer supply.

System inertia. If a project is outside the plan, there are serious difficulties in implementing it. This brings about the dampening of managerial initiatives and an unwillingness or inability to take advantage of rare opportunities since it is very difficult and thus costly to do so. The decision to conduct the unplanned Systems Engineering Teachers Training Course was made to take advantage of my services. Obtaining the necessary permission to hire me, finding the instructors to teach the course, and acquiring the computer equipment all presented serious difficulties. This adverse situation forced the ministry and the university to accept sub-optimum choices. Nevertheless, with the proper conditions—e.g., a strong and prestigious ministry, wide connections, and going through the ''back door''—the system inertia was mitigated and an acceptable solution was found.

Closed system. For a variety of reasons, China in the past experienced a semi-closed economy, with a small, though essential, foreign trade. Trade transactions, and scientific, technical and cultural exchanges, when they took place, were closely controlled. Personal contacts with foreign colleagues, travel abroad, and participation in international conferences were the exception. This strangled the free flow of scientific and technical information and of technological know-how into China. Chinese enterprise managers would rarely have the needed technical or managerial data, an understanding of such data, or even the awareness of the existence of such data to make adequate decisions in solving their problems. Thus, management was mainly restricted to the environment of China and cut off from the rest of the world.

Lack of accountability system. There is a lack of an *operational* accountability system for economic, though not political, performance from the top level down to the individual employee in an organization. Often, poor decisions and performances are blamed on China's difficult work conditions. One might expect better management to alleviate the constraints posed by unfavorable conditions, yet in China the lack of an accountability system seems to generate the opposite effect. Nobody within the ministry or the factory was held accountable for not purchasing software or technical training. Such a decision had effectively prevented the use of over one million dollars of investment for two years.

Centralized decision making and allocation of resources. In China's centrally planned economy, government organizations, and not enterprises, play the primary role in reaching strategic decisions, such as establishing corporate objectives and goals, planning and allocating resources, and formulating corporate policies. The extent of an enterprise's participation in the strategic decision-making process depends, among other things, on its relationship with its superior organizations, its relative importance and size, and the degree of centralization of the economic management system at the time.

The enterprise and its superior organization may disagree about goals and objectives and the resources needed to attain them. Still, the enterprise is expected to implement those strategic decisions, even though its low participation in the decision-making process affects its motivation in doing so. There may be fewer incentives to implement them adequately than there would be if those decisions were made jointly. The examples of the factory's poor performance in developing data processing applications and the running of the management education program at the university illustrate these points.

Foreign Trade System

The factors stemming from the foreign trade system reflect the Chinese centrally planned economic system. Yet, it is important to give them more space in view of the role foreign trade plays in the transfer of technology.

Difference of goal and interest between the foreign trade corporation and the end-user. In the case of transfer of technology to China, the foreign trade corporation's principal criterion of success is the ability to respond to the end-user's request—to satisfy his demands—with the least possible cost to itself and expenditure of foreign exchange. The effectiveness of the transfer is often barely considered. Foreign trade corporations neglect questions of post-sale technical and marketing services, personnel training, and the import and adaptation of software and know-how. The end-user, who is more apt to recognize the importance of those services, has little or no access to the supplier and little or no awareness of the services the supplier may offer. Moreover, the end-user is under tremendous pressure to please the foreign trade corporation, his only possible representative to the international technology market.

The decision not to purchase training services and software with the computer equipment is partly explained by the difference of goal and interest between the foreign trade corporation and the factory. Also, the ministry's desire to preserve its working relationship with the foreign trade corporation forced it to accede to the corporation's demand and cancel the university's original computer purchase contract.

Information network.   In the civil sector, much information concerning the availability and specifications of foreign technology enters China through foreign trade corporations: they are information gatekeepers, more frequently in contact with the suppliers than any other Chinese organizations. Combined with China's general tendency to provide information on a need-to-know basis, the corporations' control of the search for, access to and in part the diffusion of technical information constitutes an interesting factor in the balance of power between them and end-users. Also, in view of their different interests and objectives, foreign trade corporation and end-users have different uses for the same information. Yet the corporation's control over the information network often introduces distortion in the end-users' use of the information.

International trade know-how.   The concentration of foreign trade transactions through the foreign trade corporations has many advantages: closer control over imports and exports, concentration of scarce international trade skills and know-how, stronger bargaining power, a centralized information source and network, etc. One of the disadvantages is that the enterprise itself does not have the opportunity to develop foreign trade know-how. With its limited exposure to foreign trade, in its view transferring technology becomes synonymous with the transfer of equipment, at the expense of more suitable modes of transfer. Also, its understanding of the supplier/end-user relationship is static: once a commercial transaction is performed, little relationship remains in the form of post-sale services and the flow of marketing and technical data.

In the case of the purchase of the computer equipment at the university, the original choice of the microcomputer supplier was based on one single criterion: the immediate availability of the hard disk. Other crucial, marketing-type factors, as noted in chapter 5, were not considered. Also, following the delivery of the computer equipment, representatives of the university found it difficult, almost embarrassing, to establish a post-sale relationship with the supplier for fear of overstepping the proper boundary of such a relationship. In the West, such a relationship is considered both normal and desirable by both parties.

Foreign trade and technology transfer policy.   Reflecting the ideological bias for hardware over software and combined with self-reliance, the transfer of technology was equated with the transfer of equipment or turn-key plants. Hardly any provisions were made for the purchase of software, technical and management training services, and technical and managerial consulting services. The outcome of such a policy was mostly the attainment of, at best, a sub-optimum transfer. Even if such a policy were to change, foreign trade corporations would find it difficult to adapt quickly to the new transfer modes, e.g., licensing, training and consulting services and joint ventures.

Human Resources

The most important factor of all, the human resource factor, is examined along three dimensions: technical, managerial and entrepreneurship.

Technical Resources

Technical support ranges from the diagnosis of problems, to the formulation of possible technological solutions, to the search and selection of feasible technologies for solutions, to their adaptation and further development within the recipient environment. In all the cases examined in the previous chapters, technical resources were seriously lacking to the point of jeopardizing the transfer of the technology.

Note should be made of basic differences in the predisposition for using technical expertise between the factory and the university. Although the factory clearly needed technical support to develop computerized management applications, it was the university that sought technical expertise from the Chinese electronics engineer from the computer factory and myself. Moreover, the factory was reluctant to cooperate with the university to obtain badly needed technical support.[1]

China's isolation limited whatever technical support existed. For example, the Chinese computer engineer was unaware of the development and rise of microcomputers in the United States, and recommended the purchase of outdated, more expensive technology.[2] In the Systems Engineering Teachers Training Course, hundreds of instruction hours were wasted due in part to the lack of adequately trained and experienced instructors.

On the positive side, the university case has demonstrated that a rapid and successful technical resource development is possible with the presence of a minimum of favorable conditions: support from the organization leadership, proper selection of trainees and training methodology, and presence of expertise. The development of the planning and control system at the factory is a case in point. Yet more impressive was the rapid progress demonstrated by the payroll system team, which showed great technical and managerial skills and led its project to a successful end.

Management Resources

For our purposes, managerial resources are divided into the general management of an enterprise and the management of its technology.

General management.   In the cases discussed in the previous chapters, the general management did not have adequate skills and know-how to help plan, direct and control the transfer of the technology. Why? The overly centralized economic system does not foster the development of those skills and know-how. The general manager in a Chinese enterprise does not face an environment in which he is required to do long-term planning, since the plan is determined at higher levels. Also, he can muster so few resources—manpower, capital and materials, all of which are defined and fixed in the yearly plan—and control so few variables, such as prices, products or product lines, market and market channels, that it would be useless for him to set long-term objectives, strategies and plans for his enterprise. Since he does not have to do so, he naturally does not have the opportunity to develop those skills. Moreover, as noted in chapter 4, the education level and technical expertise of top management in Chinese industrial enterprise are abysmally low.

Yet, while the decision to transfer the technology is made at a higher level, the general management is culturally and politically expected to comply with that decision and manage the transfer. In addition, it has to operate under very difficult conditions: scarcity of resources and rigid bureaucratic and systemic constraints. The purchase of the computer system for the factory and the conduct of the Systems Engineering Teachers Training Course were made under those conditions. The general management feels that its superior organization shares the responsibility for the outcome of the implementation, since it is only abiding by that organization's decisions under difficult or deficient work conditions. With such a frame of mind, management usually adopts a satisfying-the-bureaucracy attitude, makes repeated demands for additional resources, feels only partially accountable for its decisions, and exhibits a lack of initiative, consulting its superiors even for minor decisions.[3]

The university and the factory leadership put constant pressure on the ministry for more resources beyond those originally allocated. The factory management felt that the ministry shared part of the blame for the delays in developing data processing applications. That feeling substantially reduced the factory's motivation to perform, which it finally did under the threat of having the computer system taken away.

Management of the technology.   Technology management acts as the linchpin between the technology and the organization, manages its transfer, and adapts and further develops it within the recipient environment. Serious difficulties are encountered in the discharge of technology management's responsibility.

Management operates under the handicap of weak technical training and lack of experience. Both computer center directors at the factory and the university, and the dean in charge of the systems engineering program (see ''Entrepreneurship'' below) had little managerial and technical training to conceive, define and perform their jobs adequately.[4] But, once positive working and training conditions are created, middle-level management, if willing, shows an ability for rapid development of both technical and managerial skills. A case in point is the impressive progress shown by the dean and the leaders of the factory and university data processing projects. Gradually, that newly acquired expertise trickled up to top management within the two organizations.

In all observed cases, technologies have been in effect transferred with varying degrees of success. Yet, the transfers were conducted inefficiently, under difficult conditions. Plans had to be revised frequently. Deadlines were met only exceptionally. Subordinates' lack of experience, initiative and authority forced higher-level management to get involved in implementation details. Its lack of authority over its own subordinates severely limited its control over implementation.[5]

Management shows a mixed ability to take advantage of technical advice because it faces systemic constraints and unfamiliar technologies. For example, contrary to advice, the Chinese preferred not to purchase computer training services and software, and conducted close to 200 hours of computer instruction in overly large classes with little regard to quality of students and teaching methodology. Yet, when the benefits of advice could be clearly demonstrated, such as in the cases of the microcomputer and of the second systems engineering course following the mixed results of the first one, the leadership was willing to take it into consideration.

Role of Individual Entrepreneurship

For an organization successfully to undertake new projects, it needs entrepreneurship to guide it into uncharted waters. Organizations receiving entirely new technologies, such as those described in the previous two chapters, in a sense embark on new ventures requiring entrepreneurs who must also possess some technical capabilities to act as transfer facilitators. To conduct the transfer of systems engineering and data processing, the university found in the person of one of the department deans the combination of an entrepreneur and a transfer facilitator, without whom the transfer could not have taken place, or would not have been as successful.

The role of the dean was extensive and touched on every single aspect of the transfer project. He represented the university in negotiations with the ministry and other organizations, including the factory. He built up the team of Chinese instructors by scouting for them across the country. Within the university, he was clearly the project leader, defining tasks, selecting the personnel, and allocating resources. He acted as the academic director of the Systems Engineering Teachers Training Course. He worked closely with me and was an effective bridge between me and the rest of the Chinese work environment. He played a key role in the selection and purchase of the microcomputers.

In the course of his work, he displayed personal qualities and skills crucial to his pivotal role. He exhibited a high achievement need. Encouraged by the new political climate, he wanted to contribute to his country's modernization. Despite his lack of formal training in management and systems engineering, he could conceptualize and direct the project and see where its implementation would lead. He seemed undaunted by the unusually centralized and rigid administrative structure, and used his superb skills to work within it and was willing to take calculated risks to work around it. He showed a resourcefulness in tapping and judiciously using scarce resources. Finally, his intellect, quick learning abilities and versatile mind compensated for his initial lack of training in modern management and systems engineering and experience in working with non-Chinese.

Type of Technology

Two aspects are considered in this section: the past experience the Chinese had with the technology, and the interaction of China's technological culture with the newly introduced technology.

Past Experience with Technology

Of the three technology transfers observed—computers, management techniques, and data processing—the first is most familiar to the Chinese. Both at the university and the factory, the imported computer equipment was, however, technologically more advanced than the state of the art in China. For example, the university's microcomputers were among the first introduced to the country. Yet, problems that the recipients' organizations experienced during the transfer of the computer equipment did not seem to originate from the Chinese unfamiliarity with the technology per se but from its management. This may be credited to the Chinese experience in computer technology, more specifically, in hardware technology.

The situation was different with the other two technologies. Modern management education had been banned for 20 years at a time when it experienced rapid development abroad. Computers were used in China for military and scientific rather than managerial purposes. Thus, data processing development and implementation were unfamiliar to the Chinese. The Chinese difficulties in transferring those technologies were even greater since, to be successful, data processing must be developed on sound management and organization principles. Moreover, with their pro-hardware bias, the Chinese were at a loss in transferring those two soft technologies efficiently. Thus, the recipients' meager familiarity with both technologies was a factor, at least initially, in the factory's difficulties with developing its data processing applications, and the university's with introducing modern management training.

Technological Culture

All three technologies were developed and have been widely used in technologically advanced societies. Those technologies fitted with the prevalent technological culture of those countries, their attitudes, mentalities and perceptions of their own environment. Living in a culture underdeveloped technologically and materially, the Chinese are unaccustomed to the daily use of high technologies so common in other societies. Thus they lack much of the technological infrastructure, attitudes, mentalities and world outlook congruent with, and supportive of, the creation and use of advanced technologies. Consequently, China's wide technological culture gap is bound to present serious obstacles to the transfer of high technology.

Two examples illustrate the effects of the wide technology gap. The payroll system developed at the university incorporated advanced data base and data processing techniques. Yet, as soon as it was successfully tested and run in parallel, it was shelved. Social and cultural factors were at play: adopting the payroll system would have created a sizeable number of redundancies in the payroll department; the system was developed merely as an exercise for the students and was perceived as being of little practical value to the university. But moreover, faced with that technology gap, the university leadership did not seem to realize the value or the advanced level of the payroll system, despite the fact that data processing was a fashionable idea throughout the country.

The technology gap also manifested itself in what I called the "Jade Buddha Temple" syndrome.[6] The university computer center director imposed stringent limitations on users' access to the facilities, claiming that such measures were necessary to protect the highly valued equipment. The usefulness (for management and computer training) of the computers to the university was thus paradoxically reduced substantially.

Foreign Consultants

The data presented in this and the previous two chapters clearly indicate the crucial role that I, as the foreign expert, played in the transfer of the three technologies—computer, data processing, and management and systems engineering education—to the university. In each of these technologies, my role spanned all stages of the transfer process, including defining the problem at hand; identifying possible technologies for its solution; searching for, and selecting, a feasible technology; transferring and adapting it to the recipient's environment; and developing technical skills. All through the transfer stages, I provided valuable services that the Chinese could not provide at the time, such as opening channels of information with other countries, explaining and interpreting foreign data to the recipients in ways that they could comprehend, and obtaining the cooperation of North American organizations.

Since software and expertise are embodied in people and take a relatively long time to transfer, my impact was more pronounced on the transfer of the "soft" technologies, i.e., management education and data processing. Also, at a time when it was inconceivable for the university to send any of its members abroad to purchase computer equipment and software and to obtain management teaching materials and books, I could perform such tasks for the university.

That impact can be recognized when contrasting the performance of organizations with access to a foreign expert to those without. The differences in the university and the factory's experiences in developing data processing, and the university's relative success in establishing a systems and industrial engineering program compared to the earlier outcome of similar efforts of its other, more prestigious Chinese counterparts are excellent examples.[7]

Apart from professional qualifications, a foreign expert, as an effective transfer facilitator, must help bridge the cultural gap that exists between his culture and that of the technology recipients. He should display at least a minimal understanding of, or sensitivity to, the recipient's environment, in order to adopt technology transfer approaches feasible in that environment. He should be aware of his professional and cultural biases, which might be detrimental to the recipient. He should help the recipient develop a technological independence, making himself less and less indispensable.

The hiring of foreign experts as transfer facilitators is one way to alleviate the effects of transfer barriers. Yet China's isolation and highly centralized and rigid administrative system have not allowed the country to devise efficient mechanisms to seek and get foreign expertise. Also, the society's ethnocentric tendencies force foreigners to its margin both socially and professionally, making it difficult to fully utilize them. Their effectiveness to Chinese employers can be improved only if the foreign consultant is accepted as a full member in the work place and systemic barriers are removed, both of which are painstakingly slow processes.

7

Conclusions

The previous three chapters described attempts to establish the field of modern management education and training in post-Mao China, and cases in the transfer of computer and computer-related technologies in a higher education institution and a factory. All three chapters presented and analyzed decisions made by the concerned organizations, emphasizing the factors that influenced and explained the decisions. The factors can be divided into two major categories. The first category includes systemic factors stemming from the Chinese culture, the characteristics of the Chinese socialist ideology and political system, the low level of economic development, the pervasive scarcity of resources, and particularly human resources. The second category includes the factors related to change: the period that this study covers was one of intense pressure for change, felt at all levels within the society, and initiated vigorously by the Chinese leadership, which claimed that the country was being ushered into a new historical stage of its socialist construction. The introduction of modern management education and training and of computer technologies was part of those changes.

The current Chinese leadership considers that the Third Plenary Session of the Central Committee of the Eleventh Party Congress, held in December 1978, marked a turning point in the history of the People's Republic of China, and a milestone in the ongoing process of change. At that meeting a new two-pronged ideological course was announced, which established the supremacy of "Seek Truth From Facts" and "Practice Is The Sole Criterion Of Truth" over the "Two Whateverisms"; it also held that China had entered a "New Historical Period," in which economic development would take precedence over class struggle (see chapter 1). A second development was building a foundation for economic readjustments and reforms of the economic and enterprise management systems. The result was the formulation and development of the eight-character economic policy: "Readjust, Reform, Consolidate and Improve."

The implications of the decisions taken at the Third Plenary are many and far-reaching. The Chinese leadership argued that the application of Marxist ideology should be made in a relativistic way, i.e., based on the environment faced rather than on the past declarations and actions of one leader or on their interpretations.

This new approach was part of the "liberation of the mind" and an attempt at shedding dogmatism and the personality cult. It could potentially lead the way to a more flexible management of the country's politics and economy. The implications of the "New Historical Period" include the fact that socialism, as a system, is entrenched in the country, that there should be less concern for chasing after counter-revolutionaries and more for national economic development. Such a position, the current Chinese leadership believed, would remedy the many politically-caused economic disruptions of the past 30 years, eliminate the need to launch political campaigns, and set the scene for a more stable environment for economic development.

The policies and reforms pertaining to enterprise management presented a number of characteristics. The principal ones are: 1) their widespread and far-reaching implications seemed to chart the enterprise management system onto a totally new course for socialist China; 2) they had the strong support of the majority of the national leadership; 3) their content and modes of implementation were still in an experimental stage; and 4) they intended to redefine the multifaceted roles and interrelationship of the State, local government, and enterprise regarding questions of resource allocation and the locus of decision-making.

The last three chapters have focused on management practices. They examined the strategy, policy and operational interactions between organizations at the local level and their superiors in the central government, the environment they faced in their daily operations, and their decision-making approaches and processes. The examination was conducted along two lines: the introduction of modern management education at the national as well as the local levels; and the introduction of high technology into organizations, principally through transfer from abroad.

In addition to learning more about post-Mao policies and reforms and about Chinese enterprise management practices, one of the principal objectives of the research is to examine the extent to which divergence and congruence existed on two levels: between leadership's pronouncements and its actions; and between national policies, i.e., the macro level, and the behavior of Chinese organizations responsible for implementing those policies, i.e., the micro level. Our findings in chapters 4, 5 and 6 point to the existence of both divergence and congruence.

Congruence and Divergence

It is clear that nationwide efforts were made to formulate and implement new policies and approaches to national development in the post-Mao era in all spheres, including the arts, literature, education, economy, and politics. In all cases Party and government organizations supported or initiated those efforts. In a centralized decision-making system such as the Chinese, no organization or institution could introduce long-term changes without at least the tacit approval of the authorities. In this respect, pronouncements of policy shifts and actual developments reflected a congruence between the pronouncements and the actions of the authorities.

Even before the consolidation of major policy shifts at the Third Plenary Session in December 1978, the central government supported Sichuan's experiment in reforming enterprise management. Also before that date, ministries began to plan for the revival of modern management education, as illustrated by the Qinhuangdao Conference held in the Summer of 1978. The central government provided crucial support for the establishment or re-establishment of management education and training programs, and for the setting up of professional management associations. The mechanism for a massive technology transfer was initiated, as indicated by the sizeable increase of China's foreign trade figures of 1978 and 1979 and the restructuring of the foreign trade system. The government approved increased contacts with foreign institutions or individuals in business, education, government, and professional circles, for the purpose of transferring technologies and learning from foreign experiences.

Reflecting China's highly centralized administrative structure, government efforts at the national level soon translated into actions within local organizations. Both the factory and the university displayed a close working relationship with the ministry in Beijing. In the cases of establishing the Systems Engineering Teachers Training Course and introducing computer and data processing technology and know-how, that relationship translated into the ministry's directives, provision of resources, and supervision. We also noted the university and factory's strong willingness to cooperate with the ministry, although the performance of the factory was mixed for reasons detailed in chapters 5 and 6.

Overall, the degree of congruence between the central government and local organizations, particularly if those organizations are directly under the jurisdiction of central government offices, is expected to be high in a highly centralized economic and political system. The center largely controls the allocation of resources and the appointment of top-level cadre in the local organizations; thus, the organizations should be considered extensions of the center: its operating arms.

Yet there are also divergences between the authorities' pronouncements and their actions, as well as between actions and behavior at the center and at the local level. To illustrate the first type of divergence, we noted in chapter 4 the inadequate allocation of resources at the national level for the development of modern management education, particularly for academic programs, and the lack of financial support, for training abroad. This diverged from the repeated statements of intention made by the leadership indicating a desire to move enterprise management from a backward to a modern state. And backward it was, since in 1978 management education, training and research had practically no institutional structure and support following a 20-year ban. Whether due to system inertia—e.g., administrative or ideological (primacy of technology, or production forces, over management, or relations of production); to lack of experience and a solid base to build from (realizing the important role of enterprise management in the country's modernization, yet having difficulties in developing appropriate plans and implementing them); to lack of resources, particularly human and financial resources;

or simply to the leadership's neglect, government actions did not seem commensurate with their stated policies regarding the development of management education and training.[1]

Differences existed between the macro level and the micro level along two dimensions: the divergence between policy pronouncements at the national level and their implementation at the local level, caused principally by environmental and systemic factors; and that caused by inherent differences between the two levels.

A large number of environmental and systemic factors that explained the divergence between the macro and the micro level were mentioned in the cases of the establishment of management education programs, the importation of computers, and the introduction and development of data processing. Constant pressure put on the Chinese decision makers to undertake projects, knowing full well that only sub-optimum results could be expected because of scarcity of resources, or their inefficient use contributed to that divergence. For example, the decision to hold the course at the time and in the way it was held was made hastily in order to take advantage of the availability of scarce resources (the presence of a foreign expert) without due consideration of other similarly important factors, such as the presence of computer equipment, teaching materials, and instructors. The efficient conduct of the course was hindered by delays in the delivery of the computer equipment because of bureaucratic infighting. Pedagogical inclinations based on Confucian approaches to education prevalent in China were not suitable to the needs of the course. Perceived political and ideological constraints, combined with poor foreign language training, did not allow efficient use of the teaching materials brought from abroad.

The factory's attempts at developing data processing applications were tremendously hindered by established transfer of technology practices, i.e., practical disregard for software and training, coupled with a narrow interpretation of self-reliance. China's technological culture and economic factors—ratio of capital and labor costs—were the primary reasons for shelving an advanced computerized payroll system, which also provided a data base crucial to the computerization of the management of the university, notwithstanding the university leadership's repeated statements of intent to computerize. In the final analysis, the actual barrier to the introduction of data processing at the university was not the absence of technical skills—in chapter 5, we noted the payroll project team's surprisingly rapid acquisition of technical and managerial skills—but the inadequacy of systemic factors.

Thus, systemic factors have introduced a dichotomy between policies and programs at the macro level and their implementation at the micro level. The systems engineering course did not result in the expected transfer of knowledge and particularly expertise. For many years, the factory's importation of a computer did not produce the expected computerized production management system. And the management modernization policy experienced a setback at the university when the payroll and its data base systems were shelved. But, as a foundation and experience for developing subsequent management training programs, the course may be considered successful. Subsequent programs undertaken by the university have demonstrated a high degree of success. Also, eventually, the factory began to use the computer equipment for its originally intended purpose. And the development of the payroll system, though not adopted, provided an invaluable training opportunity.

The above findings point to questions regarding China's transfer of technology, for which there seem to be no easy answers. Some of these questions are:

> Is there a congruence between the economic and managerial systems prevalent in China, and basic environmental requirements for a reasonably successful transfer of advanced technologies? If not, what systemic changes should be introduced to avoid the problems encountered in the management of the transfer, as documented in previous chapters?
>
> In view of the scarcity of resources and the technological gap that exists between China and economically developed countries, should an attempt be made at transferring advanced or intermediate, possibly more appropriate, technologies? In the case of China, what could the determinant factors be: inherent characteristics of the technology; the technological gap for a particular technology; the availability of managerial and technical skills; the shape of the learning curve; the degree of accessibility of the technology; its adaptation and innovation capabilities; economic and market factors; the characteristics of the economic and enterprise management systems; the perceived importance of the technology to Chinese decision makers; and so on?

Divergences between the macro and micro levels exist along a second dimension; that is, they result from inherent differences of interest and perspective, among various groups. Both at the factory and the university, the preservation of entrenched interests within the management hindered the introduction of new technologies. For example, both at the university and the factory new centers of power (e.g., the computer center), created with the introduction of a new technology, worked, at least in part, to benefit themselves at the expense of properly introducing the technology. Thus, the presence of interest groups within the organization had an impact on its ability to perform according to the central authorities' expectations.

Differences of interest existed between organizations and their superior at the center. The center pressured the organizations to perform with what they considered to be inadequate resources. The center's objective was to minimize resources allocated, while the organizations desired to maximize them. As a result, the organizations, as we discussed in chapter 5, requested additional resources after the start of the project, suggesting that they were needed for its completion.[2]

The center had a national perspective in its decision making, which organizations may have lacked. For example, at the ministry's request, the university reluctantly accepted students in the systems engineering course who did not have the necessary prerequisites. Those students came from organizations under the ministry, which was under pressure to have as many organizations as possible represented in the course. For that same reason, the ministry argued for large-size classes, while the university pointed out their negative effects on training efficiency.[3]

It is important to recognize that post-Mao policies have faced a dialectical framework of change and continuity. On the one hand, the pressure for change paradoxically was built up over the years by the Chinese politico-economic system itself. The system lacked adequate mechanisms to respond effectively to growing needs for political, economic, and social changes with a minimum of disturbance and at acceptable social costs. But for the process of change to be triggered, the country had to wait for the death of Mao Ze-dong and the removal of the Gang of Four from power. Yet, as expected, not only did the established system present a strong resistance to change and raise serious barriers to the introduction of change, but it also shaped and limited the formulation, mode of introduction, nature, and extent of that change. That is the dilemma that China faces in the implementation of the reforms.

On the other hand, few centrally planned economies had contemplated, let alone introduced, such systemic reforms in the political, educational, artistic, social, legal, economic and foreign trade spheres. Also, the reforms were institutionalized, thus becoming part of the system itself. The dialectical relationship between the contending as well as mutually-generated forces of change and those of the established system existed within all Chinese organizations, as illustrated in chapters 4 and 5.

Naturally, the current Chinese reformers are more apt to stress the change, in view of their biases and the interests they represent. Yet even a cursory examination of the implementation of the policies indicates that it would be a mistake to underestimate the factors of continuity and their powerful influence. Such factors and their direct impact on the reforms have been mentioned above. Of interest to an observer of China's management reforms, the presence of contending forces of continuity and change seems less important than the dynamics that govern those forces and the direction in which they are propelling the country.

Appendix 1

Curriculum of
the Industrial Engineering Undergraduate Program:
The Harbin Institute of Technology

This a draft of the Harbin Institute of Technology's curriculum for the four-year undergraduate program in the Industrial Engineering established in 1979, as presented to me in the fall of 1979. It includes required and elective courses and shows the estimate of instruction time per course, in hours.

Course Description	Instruction In Hours
I. Required Courses	
1. History of the Chinese Communist Party	90
2. Political Economics	90
3. Philosophy	90
4. Foreign Language	240
5. Physical Education	120
6. Mathematics	270
7. Physics	240
8. Chemistry	75
9. Computer Principles	60
10. Computing Language and Programming	110
11. Electrical Engineering and Electronics	160
12. Foundations of Automatic Control	60
13. Probability	50
14. Linear Algebra and Algorithm	50
15. Operations Research	50
16. Mathematical and Applied Statistics	90
17. Drafting	80
18. Mechanics	100
19. Foundations of Machinery Design	70
20. Metal Technologies	100
21. Material Dialectics	60
22. Economic and Business Law	20
23. Accounting Principles	30
24. Theory of Industrial Management and Economics	50
25. Operations Management	60
26. Systems Engineering	40

27. Engineering Economics	50
28. Production Organization	100
29. Quality Control	30
TOTAL (Required Courses)	2,635

II. Elective Courses

1. Seminar in Foreign Enterprise Management	20
2. Second Foreign Language	100
3. Factory Design	30
4. Special Questions in Economic Theory	20
5. New Technologies, Processes and Materials	20
6. Labor Psychology	20

Appendix 2

Draft of the Curriculum of
the Industrial Engineering Undergraduate Program:
Qinhuangdao Conference—Summer 1978

This is a draft of the curriculum of the four-year undergraduate program in Industrial Engineering, which was adopted by the Industrial Engineering Conference held in Qinhuangdao, Hebei Province, in the summer of 1978.

1. Political Studies
2. Physical Education
3. Foreign Language
4. Mathematics
5. Physics
6. Chemistry
7. Drafting
8. Electrical Engineering and Electronics
9. Mechanics
10. Mechanical Design
11. Metal Working
12. Metal, Materials and Heat Treatment
13. Machine Tools and Cutters
14. Machine-Building Techniques
15. Computers: Principles and Applications
16. Applied Mathematics (Operations Research, Probability and Statistics)
17. Industrial Statistics
18. Engineering Economics
19. Production Organization
20. Introduction to Enterprise Management
21. Quality Control
22. Materials Management
23. Labor Management
24. Equipment Management
25. Economic Management

In addition to the above required courses, it was suggested that the following three elective courses be offered:

1. Foreign Enterprise Management
2. Labor Psychology
3. Second Foreign Language

Three projects were included in the curriculum. The successful completion of the last two projects was a requirement for graduation.

1. Mechanical Part Project
2. Technical Design Project
3. Production Organization Project

Appendix 3

Outline of
a Short-term Training Course for
Leading Enterprise Cadre

The following is the outline of a short-term executive management training course developed for the top leadership of machine-building enterprises, principally under the First Ministry of Machine-Building. The course was developed in the first half of 1979 by faculty in one of the universities under the First Ministry.

	Instruction Hours
I. Management of State-owned Machine-Building Enterprises	
1. Introduction to Enterprise Management	14
2. Labor Quotas	8
3. Introduction to the Management of the Plan	8
4. Unified Planning Methodology	8
5. Production Technology Arrangements	10
6. Production Planning	16
7. Operations Management and Planning	28
8. Labor Management	8
9. Equipment Management	12
10. Materials Management	12
11. Total Quality Control	30
12. Economic Management	26
Subtotal	180
II. Special Discussions on Management Modernization	14
III. Special Discussions on Technology Economics	28
IV. Statistics for Machine-Building Enterprises	
1. The Meaning and Task of Statistics	2
2. Principal Statistical Methods	8
3. Production Quantity Statistics	3
4. Production Variety Statistics	1
5. Production Quality Statistics	2
6. Labor Productivity Statistics	2
7. Raw Materials, Fuels and Power Consumption Statistics	3

8. Flow of Funds Statistics		2.5
9. Cost of Production Statistics		2.5
10. Profit Statistics		2
11. Statistical Analysis		4
	Subtotal	32

V. Computers and Management

1. Introduction to Computers		6
2. Elementary Introduction to Computer Languages		8
3. Total Process of Computerized Solutions to Practical Production Problems		4
4. Management Applications of Computers		2
	Subtotal	20
	TOTAL	274

Appendix 4

Lecture Materials Presented at the First Executive Management Training Course Sponsored by the China Enterprise Management Association, March 1979

The first national professional management association in China, the China Enterprise Management Association, was established under the sponsorship of the powerful State Economic Commission in March 1979. On the day of its formal establishment, the first senior executive training course was also inaugurated. Course participants were senior executives responsible for the implementation and management of the economic plan. The following is a list of the titles and authors of the lecture materials used in the course. Without exception, the authors were distinguished scholars in their respective fields, or senior government officials.

Appendix 5

Basic Knowledge of
Industrial Economics and Enterprise Management:
Television Lecture Series

In the spring and summer of 1980, a series of lectures on economics and management were broadcast on national television under the sponsorship of the All-China Federation of Trade Unions, the Central Television Broadcasting Company, and the Editorial Board of *Jingji Guanli* (*Economic Management*) magazine. The series was titled "Basic Knowledge of Industrial Economics and Enterprise Management," and it was rebroadcast in many regions in China. One million eight hundred thousand copies of the series transcripts sold out soon after their publication. Following is the list of lecture titles of the series.

I. Basic Knowledge of Industrial Economics

 1. China-type Socialist Modernization and Readjustment of the Economic Structure.
 2. Systems of Industrial Management
 3. Plan Regulation and Market Regulation [of the Economy]
 4. Overall Arrangement of Industrial Productive Forces
 5. Industrial Specialization and Cooperation
 6. Inportation of Industrial Technology
 7. Basic Design of Industrial Enterprise
 8. Rational Utilization of Resources
 9. Industrial Production and Environmental Protection
10. Thirty Years of Arduous Undertakings

II. Basic Knowledge of Enterprise Management

 1. An Introduction to the Management of Industrial Enterprises
 2. Democratic Management of Industrial Enterprises
 3. The Management of the Plan in Industrial Enterprises
 4. Production Management in Industrial Enterprises
 5. Materials Management in Industrial Enterprises
 6. Labor Management in Industrial Enterprises
 7. Quality Control in Industrial Enterprises
 8. Management of Technology in Industrial Enterprises
 9. Equipment Management in Industrial Enterprises
10. Economic Accounting in Industrial Enterprises
11. Applications of Computers in Enterprise Management
12. Basic Knowledge of Systems Engineering

Notes

Chapter 1

1. Qinming Day is a memorial day when the Chinese people remember their dead.

2. A number of Chinese leaders were attacked openly and directly. Attacks on Mao, though more subtle, were also witnessed.

3. One of the poems posted on the Monument to the People's Heroes succinctly summarized the demonstrators' feelings of indignity about the attacks against the late premier Zhou En-lai:

   > In my grief I hear demons shriek:
   > I weep while wolves and jackals laugh.
   > Though tears I shed to mourn a hero,
   > With head raised high, I draw my sword.

   This poem was alleged to have been considered the most counterrevolutionary by the authorities at that time.

4. It was clear that Mao's relationship with members of the Gang of Four was not antagonistic but just the opposite. His political leanings were close to those of the Four. Thus, these highly selective quotations could not but raise questions in the minds of knowledgeable and independent-thinking people.

5. The best known of such pronouncements was: "With you in charge, I am at ease," which Mao allegedly said to Hua, and which was used to legitimize the latter's succession. I heard many Chinese question the constitutionality of this selection process, and even the authenticity or intent of that sentence.

6. The cliches or slogans in this paragraph were widely used in China at that time.

7. The concept of the Four Modernizations Program had been introduced twice before by the late Premier Zhou En-lai, first at the Third National People's Congress in December 1964 and later at the Fourth National People's Congress in January 1975. But in neither case was the Four Modernizations Program presented in more than a general outline, nor was it implemented, due to the political upheavals that followed.

8. *Documents of the First Session of the Fifth National People's Congress of the People's Republic of China* (Beijing: Foreign Languages Press, 1978), pp. 35–36. A fairly detailed draft outline of the Four Modernizations Program was included in a government report titled "Unite and Strive to Build a Modern, Powerful Socialist Country," the text of a speech delivered by Hua Guo-feng at the Congress on February 26, 1978. This report is included in *Documents* (to be referred to as *Documents I*), pp. 1–118.

9. Such an argument appeared in the Chinese media, and was seriously defended to me by many of my Chinese acquaintances in 1977 and 1978, who cited a few comparable Japanese and Chinese production figures in the 1950s in support of their argument. Such a view reflected the sincere desire of many Chinese to develop their economy, their firm confidence in their ability to do so, and their sad recognition that China had not performed as well as Japan. But their argument was built on shaky ground. The mere comparability of some production figures in two countries does not in itself lead to similar economic experiences.

10. *Documents I*, pp. 35–50.

11. The motto "Take steel as the key link" still occupied a privileged place in the minds of the Chinese leaders, and was part of the Four Modernizations Program. It had been used since the mid-1950s, and was inspired by Soviet developmental policies then.

12. *Documents I*, pp. 35–42 and pp. 50–55.

13. Such an opinion was shared with me by many Chinese economists, and was echoed in the national press.

14. A Chinese friend of mine, who lived in Sichuan Province in 1964 and 1965, was shocked to notice a marked reduction in the standard of living there when he returned for a visit in 1977 after an absence of 12 years.

15. *Documents I*, p. 21.

16. To some of my Chinese acquaintances, the argument went even further: a truly socialist system allowed the economic development of the country and the improvement of the people's livelihood: it did not permit a state of poverty like the "socialist system" the Gang of Four allegedly promoted. Many of my Chinese friends confided to me that: "We say that socialism is superior to capitalism. Being superior means that it should provide a better social, cultural and material life for the people. We do not want a socialism that cannot do that."

17. For a brief introduction to the notion of profit in a socialist economy, refer to Marx and Engels's *The Critique of the Gotha Program.*

18. The "Hundred Flowers" Campaign, for short, was launched by the Chinese authorities in 1956. Its stated purpose was to encourage the people to express themselves artistically and politically, and give their feedback to the leaders on the seven years of communist rule that had just passed. What those leaders heard and saw in response made them unleash the "Anti-Rightist" Campaign, in the course of which hundreds of thousands of people suffered.

19. This freedom of expression was limited to the purpose of the country's modernization needs, and was not upheld for its intrinsic value. One was free to express oneself as long as abiding by the four basic principles: follow socialism; adopt Marxism-Leninism-Mao Ze-dong Thought; accept the undisputed leadership of the Chinese Communist Party; and exercise the dictatorship of the proletariat. Not only did such a requirement limit the range of thoughts that could be expressed openly, but it also raised a crucial practical problem: who was to judge whether any of the four principles had been violated, and using what criteria and standards? Such questions were very much on the minds of Chinese leaders, many of whom had suffered in one political campaign or another, particularly the Cultural Revolution, which had subsequently been officially characterized as a time of a "feudal fascist dictatorship." But more crucially, these questions were of great concern to the intellectuals and artists, whose political power was negligible.

20. The Ministry of Education's 1981-90 plan is to double university enrollment to 2.2 million students and increase the number of higher education institutions from 700 to 1,100. This mammoth effort will raise the proportion of higher education graduates from the current 0.5 percent to 2.9 percent of the work force. Yet such a proportion does not compare favorably with other

countries: the *current* figures are 2.2 percent for Thailand, 5.5 percent for Japan, and 10.4 percent for South Korea. "China's Labor System," *The China Business Review,* vol. 8, no. 5, September-October 1981.

21. Shao-chuan Leng. "The Chinese Judicial System: A New Direction," in S.L. Greenblatt, R.W. Wilson, and A.A. Wilson, *Organizational Behavior in Chinese Society* (New York: Praeger, 1981).

22. Criminals and counterrevolutionaries, to name two, constituted other "stinking categories."

23. While it is clear that their involvement in manual labor disrupted the normal conduct of their work and that it was implemented in ways that left a lot to be desired, intellectuals had mixed reactions to this personal experience. Some were not willing to talk about it, while others said that, through it, they gained a deeper understanding of their society.

24. In the euphoria of the National Day festivities on October 1, 1977, the first to be held after the removal of the Gang of Four from power, one educator told me that the Chinese were celebrating the liberation of their minds, which was more important than the political liberation of 1949.

25. Hu Qiao-mu, "Act in Accordance with Economic Laws, Step Up the Four Modernizations," Xinhua News Agency, October 5, 1978.

26. One reason was the lack of an adequate and accurate national statistical system essential for a planned economy.

27. Later Hua Guo-feng was blamed for pushing such a high rate of economic growth and was accused of committing leftist mistakes (cf. "On Questions of Party History, *Beijing Review,* vol. 24, no. 27, July 6, 1981, p. 26).

28. Three of the many articles in the Chinese media that treated this question were: Editorial, "Zhengque renshi xin de bazi fangzhen" ("Correctly Understand the New Eight-Character Policy"), *Jingji Guangli* (*Economic Management*), issue no. 6, 1979; Shi Zheng-wen, "Readjusting the National Economy: Why and How?, *Beijing Review,* vol. 22, no. 26, June 29, 1979; and Xia Zhen, "A New Strategy for Economic Development," *Beijing Review,* vol. 24, no. 32, August 10, 1981.

29. Reported in *The China Business Review,* vol. 8, no. 4, July-August 1981, p. 6.

30. "Personal Income in China," *The China Business Review,* vol. 8, no. 2, March-April 1981, p. 20.

31. According to the World Bank report on the Chinese economy, reported in *The Chinese Business Review,* vol. 8, no. 4, July-August 1981, China's energy consumption per dollar GNP is about triple the average of that of both developing countries and industrialized market economies.

32. For more information on the structure and management of the Chinese economy, refer to Audrey Donnithorne, *China's Economic System* (London: Praeger, 1967); Joan Robinson, *Economic Management in China,* 2nd ed. (London: Anglo-Chinese Educational Institute, 1975); Dwight H. Perkins, *Market Control and Planning in Communist China* (Cambridge, Mass.: Harvard University Press, 1966); and articles by Yuan-li Wu, Thomas G. Rawski, Nicholas R. Lardy, and Frederic W. Crook in *An Economic Profile of Mainland China* and *China: A Reassessment of the Economy* (Washington, D.C.: U.S. Government Printing Office, 1967 and 1975, respectively).

33. For example, it was calculated that in 1978 depreciation funds retained by the Anshan Steel Complex, the largest in China, came to less than 1.5 percent of the assets. This proportion is clearly inadequate. Data from personal notes.

34. Based on discussions with two noted Chinese economists, Ma Hong and Xue Mu-qiao, in July 1979, in Beijing.

35. Notable was the decision to build the Baoshan Iron and Steel Complex. Cf. J.Y. Battat, "The Steel Monster," Unpublished Newsletter, Institute of Current World Affairs, April 28, 1981.

36. For instance, a chemical factory might come under the direct supervision both of a department within the Ministry of Chemical Industry and of an industrial department in the local government. It also has to comply with the decisions and regulations of a number of local bureaucracies, such as the labor and financial bureaus.

37. *New York Times,* December 26, 1978.

38. Xu Zhi-fan and Zhou Jing-hua, "Economic Policies in Rural Areas," *Beijing Review,* vol. 22, no. 16, April 20, 1979.

39. This important shift in China's policy towards accepting foreign investment underlined the seriousness of those bottlenecks and the need to alleviate them.

40. Naturally, such measures created inflationary pressures, especially after 1979 (cf. table 1).

41. At a lecture I attended in December 1979 in Beijing, a vice-chairman of the State Planning Commission stated that China could increase its industrial output by 30 percent without adding one piece of new equipment, using existing production capacity and better management.

42. They included the State Financial and Economic Commission (established in 1979), the State Agricultural Commission (1979), the State Machine-Building Commission (1980), the State Foreign Investment Control/Import-Export Commission (1979), the State Energy Commission (1980). In early 1981, the State Council Economic Readjustment Office and the State Council Office for the Reform of the Management System were established, replacing the Financial and Economic Commission.

43. Xue Mu-qiao's view was that China's economy was a socialist one, in the sense that almost all the productive assets were socially owned—either State-owned, mainly in industry, or collectively-owned, mainly in agriculture—and that it was regulated by a central plan. Yet, since it was also a commodity economy, it would be wrong to negate the need for a market regulator. He has elaborated those views in a number of articles and speeches, a selection of which was published in a book titled *Dangqian Woguo Jingji Ruogan Wenti* (*Certain Current Problems in Our National Economy*), (Beijing: People's Publishing House, 1980).

44. Comment made by Vice-Premier Bo Yi-bo, reported in *Xinhua News Agency Bulletin,* September 29, 1981.

45. Ibid.

46. *Xinhua News Agency Bulletin,* March 1, 1981, p. 3.

47. Xue Mu-qiao had often used this example to stress the need for enterprise integration, e.g., processing enterprises in urban areas with those producing raw materials in the countryside. Such a move would prevent rural enterprises from retaining raw materials to produce finished products less efficiently than their urban counterparts. It is interesting to note that had the market elements advocated by Xue been in place and operational within the Chinese economy, such a situation would not have existed: inefficient enterprises could not survive in a competitive market. See "More on Economic Reform," *Beijing Review,* vol. 23, no. 36, September 8, 1981.

48. Information on this strategy was obtained during interviews conducted in Shanghai in August and September 1980 with leaders of the Office of Enterprise Management of the State Economic Policy, Shanghai Municipality, and a number of Chinese economists.

49. See table 1. The Retail Price Index is a composite index of State listed prices, negotiated industrial prices, and rural market prices indexes. It undervalues the consumer price index.

50. *Xinhua News Agency Bulletin,* December 8 and 13, 1980.

51. A more rational energy use consists principally of reducing the high level of waste through conservation, and of switching to coal, a more abundant and cheaper source of energy.

52. See "Current Economic Situation on the Chinese Mainland," *Issues and Studies,* Taipei, vol. 17, no. 10, October 1981, p. 10.

53. First Vice-Premier Wan Li went on a 40-day investigation tour, visiting 10 major ports and 17 railway lines. See "Style of Work," *Beijing Review,* vol. 24, no. 44, November 2, 1981, p. 3.

54. See Bo Yi-bo in *Xinhua News Agency Bulletin,* September 29, 1981. Also, actions such as the resumption of the Baoshan Iron and Steel Complex indicate the partial success of the heavy industry lobby in late 1981.

Chapter 2

1. For more information on the socialist transformation of China's economy, refer to Hsueh Mu-chiao [Xue Mu-qiao] et al. *The Socialist Transformation of the National Economy in China.* Foreign Languages Press, 1960); A. Donnithorne, *China's Economic System* (London: Praeger, 1967); A. Eckstein, *China's Economic Revolution* (Cambridge: Cambridge University Press 1977); and *Weida de Shinian (Ten Great Years)* (Beijing: 1959).

2. Zhou Zhun-hua, "Lun Woguo Shehuizhuyi Gongyouzhi de Zhudao Diwei yu Gaige Tujing" (On the Leading Position of, and Ways of Reforming, Our Socialist Public Ownership), *Jingji Kexue (Economic Science),* no. 1, 1982.

3. For citations on China's economic system see note 32, Chapter 1.

4. Zhang Shu-guang, "Reform the Economic Structure and Increase the Macroeconomic Results," *Social Sciences in China,* no. 1, 1982; and personal notes.

5. "State Council Announces Decisions on Rural Collective Enterprises," *Xinhua News Agency Bulletin,* Beijing, May 17, 1981.

6. See W. Brugger, *Democracy and Organization in the Chinese Industrial Enterprise, 1948-1953* (Cambridge: Cambridge University Press, 1976); R.M. Richman, *Industrial Society in Communist China* (New York; 1969); *Zhongguo Shehuizhuyi Gongye Qiye Guanli (China's Socialist Industrial Enterprise Management)* (Beijing: People's University Press, 1980); *Shehuizhuyi Gongye Qiye Guanli (Socialist Industrial Enterprise Management)* (Shanghai: People's Publishing House, 1980).

7. S. Andors, *China's Industrial Revolution* (New York: Pantheon, 1977).

8. Based on a presentation made by a vice-chairman of the State Planning Commission in Beijing, summer 1978.

9. Data on the Sichuan experiment were extracted from the following sources: Ren Tao, "What Are the Reasons for the Rapid Success of Sichuan Province's 100 Experimental Enterprises?" *Jingji Guanli (Economic Management),* December 1979; Lin Ling, "The Situation of Sichuan Province's Experiment in Expanding the Enterprise Right for Self-Management in the Last Year," *Jingji Guanli (Economic Management),* June 1980; Lin Ling, "Experiences and Problems of the Reform of the Economic System of Sichuan Province in the Last Two Years" *Jingji Guanli (Economic Management),* June 1981; Tian Yun, "More Authority for Enterprises Revives the Economy," *Beijing Review,* April 6, 1981; Wolfgang Kasper, "Note on the Sichuan Experiment," *The Australian Journal of Chinese Affairs,* no. 7, 1982.

10. Data on the eight-enterprise experiment are from personal notes.

11. Gu Zong-chang, "Guanyu Guoying Qiye Zifuyunkui de Jige Wenti" (Problems in State-Owned Enterprises' Responsibility for Profits and Losses), *Jingji Guanli (Economic Management)*, December 1980.

12. I collected the data on this section of "Zifuyunkui" in interviews conducted in late August and early September 1980 with official representatives of the Office of Enterprise Management of the State Economic Commission, Shanghai Muncipality; of the Shanghai Diesel Engine Plant; and of the Shanghai Institute of Mechanical Engineering.

13. Five taxes were imposed: an income tax, a real estate tax (or rent), a transportation vehicles tax, a value added tax (previously the industrial and commercial tax) and an adjustment tax (to adjust a wide range of rates of profits between industrial sectors). Two additional fees were imposed for interest paid on fixed capital and on working capital provided by the State.

14. The debate on whether or not a system of enterprise responsibility for profits and losses can and should be implemented in State-owned enterprises in China's socialist economy resurfaced in the first part of 1979 with articles by Luo Jing-fen, "Quanmin Suoyouzhi Qiye Keyi Shixing Zifuyunkui" (Enterprises Owned by the Whole People May Implement [the System of] "Responsibility for Profits and Losses"), Wu Kai-tai, "Quanmin Suoyouzhi Qiye Bu Neng Shixing Zifuyunkui" (Enterprises Owned by the Whole People Cannot Implement [No System of] Responsibility for Profits and Losses), "Quanmin Suoyouzhi Qiye Shixing Zifuyunkui Shi Ge Hao Banfa" (To Implement [the System of] Responsibility for Profits and Losses in Enterprises Owned by the Whole People Is a Good Measure), *Jingji Guanli (Economic Management)*, no. 6, no. 9 and no. 9, respectively, 1979.

15. Lin Ling, "Experiences and Problems of the Reform."

16. See note 12 above.

17. Lin Ling, "Experiences and Problems of the Reform."

18. "Outline Report on the National Forum on Reforming the Industrial Management System Issued by the State Economic Commission and the State Council Office for the Reform of the Management System (March 14, 1981)" in *Issues and Studies*, Taipei, April 1982.

19. From personal notes.

20. "Outline Report on the National Forum."

21. Tian Yun, "More Authority for Enterprises," and "Sichuansheng Kuoda Qiye Zizhuquan ba Qiye Gaohuo le" (Expanding Enterprises' Right for Self-Management Has Revived Enterprises in Sichuan Province), in *1981—Gongye Jingying Guanli Jingyan Xuanbian (Selections on Industrial Management Experiences—1981)* (Beijing: People's Publishing House, 1981).

22. "Outline Report on the National Forum." It is interesting to note that in 1980 China's total industrial output value increased by 8.7 percent over the previous year. This growth rate was broken down into a 1.4 percent increase in heavy industry and an 18.4 percent increase in light industry. Without more detail available about the sectorial composition of the 5,777 industrial enterprises, it is difficult to assess their aggregate performance (a 6.8 percent increase) against the performance of the rest of the country.

23. "Shanghaishi Kuoquan Shidian de Xiaoguo he Tihui" (Results and Experience of the Experiment of Expanding the Right [for Self-Management] in Shanghai Muncipality) and "Beijingshi Jiaqiang dui Kuoquan Qiye de Lingdao, Chongfen Fahui Jingji Zhengce de Weili" (Beijing Muncipality Strengthens the Leadership of [the Experiment] of Expanding the Enterprise Right for Self-Management, [and] Gives Full Play to the Power of the Economic Policy), in *Selections on Industrial Management*.

24. Ma Quan-shan, et al. "Zai Wenbu Fazhanzhong Zhubu Wanshan Gongye Jingji Zerenzhi" ("Gradually Perfect the System of Industrial Economic Responsibility in the Course of Steady Development"), *Jingji Yanjiu (Economic Studies)*, No. 2, 1982.

25. Derived from Ma Quan-shan ("Gradually Perfect the System").

26. The Chinese authorities pressed their enterprises to "act according to economic laws." Enterprises shifting production to the more profitable product lines acted, indeed, according to economic laws. Yet the authorities were displeased with the resulting shortages in the less profitable product lines and tried to remedy the problem using administrative (plan), rather than economic (price incentives) mechanisms. This example illustrates one of the weakest and most contradictory aspects of the reforms, and their dilemmas.

27. "A Boom-to-Bust TV Saga," *China Business Review*, July-August 1981.

28. "Outline Report on the National Forum."

29. In 1980, 6,000 State-owned industrial enterprises, or 15 percent of the total, were part of the experiment. They produced 60 percent of the total output value and 70 percent of the total profits in industry.

30. I derived the negative growth rates of those Shanghai industrial enterprises not taking part in the experiments from the data provided in "Shanghaishi Kuoquan Shidian de Xiaoguo he Tihui" in *Selections on Industrial Management Experiences—1981*.

31. Questions as to the design of the experiments and their political and economic implications, and whether enterprises can be truly independent accounting units and responsible for their profits and losses were discussed during my interviews in Shanghai in 1980 (see note 12 above). Also, refer to note 14 in this chapter.

Chapter 3

1. Farmer and Richman's environmental constraints model includes four broad categories of variables: educational, sociological-cultural, political-legal, and economic. For more information, see Richard Farmer and Barry Richman, *Comparative Management and Economic Progress*, rev. ed. (Bloomington, Ind.: Cedarwood, 1970).

2. Michael H. Agar, *The Professional Stranger*, New York: Academic Press, 1980). p. 203.

3. Ibid., p. 40.

4. A Chinese family lacks the amenities typically available to a family in the West. Poor kitchen facilities, lack of appliances and a yet-to-be-developed food industry make the preparation of a meal in China an arduous and time-consuming task.

5. With the gradual improvement of the standard of living, including the availability of fast food restaurants, better food marketing and gas stoves in new housing, it will be interesting to look into this lunch break question a few years from now.

6. Agar, p. 50.

7. Ibid.

8. Dennison Nash, "The Ethnologist as Stranger," *Southwestern Journal of Anthropology* 19 (1963): 149-67.

9. In early 1978, in response to foreign students' requests to travel within China, visit factories and communes, and get to see the country outside the university gates, the Ministry of Education made public the newly established policy on foreign students' extracurricular activities:

Students were in China to study, and only token, limited extracurricular activities would be permitted.

10. Agar, pp. 54-55 and 58.

11. Canada's foreign policy, and more specifically its China policy, was considered to be positive in Chinese foreign affairs circles. Also, and more importantly, China has a Canadian hero. He is Dr. Norman Bethune, a military surgeon, who went to China in the mid-1930s and offered his professional services to the Communist forces. His death less than two years after his arrival there was considered the ultimate sacrifice made for the Chinese revolution.

12. Arthur J. Vidich, "Participant Observer and the Collection and Interpretation of Data," in William J. Filstead, ed, *Qualitative Methodology* (Chicago, Ill.: Markham Publishing Company, 1970).

Chapter 4

1. Unless otherwise indicated, data for this chapter are from personal notes, and, in most cases, were collected from primary sources.

2. The history of management education at HIT was told to me in the course of many discussions in 1979 with HIT's faculty and administrators who have been closely involved in that field. I reconstructed the history from my interviewees' reminiscences, since, I was told, all records prior to the Cultural Revolution were lost. This account of the development of management education at HIT may be the only (reconstructed) written record of this chapter of HIT's history.

3. It was not clear whether the 30 members of the three research groups were part of the 36 faculty, or in addition to them. My guess, based on the organization of research and teaching personnel in Chinese universities, is that almost all, if not all, of the 30 were part of the 36.

4. In the "Afterword" of *Zhongguo Shehuizhuyi Guoying Gongye Qiye Guanli (China's Socialist State-owned Industrial Enterprise Management),* 2nd ed. (Beijing, 1980).

5. Franz Schurmann, *Ideology and Organization in Communist China,* 2nd ed. (Berkeley, Calif.: University of California Press, 1968).

6. For an excellent discussion of this point, see Schurmann.

7. Huan Xiang, "Cong Guanli Dao Jingli" (From Bureaucrat to Manager), *Jingji Guanli (Economic Management),* November 1980.

8. Hua Luo-geng, an eminent applied mathematician and considered the father of China's operations research, was instrumental in attempting to introduce O.R. in Chinese organizations. He was severely criticized and suffered during the Cultural Revolution.

9. The five economic research institutes were the Institutes of Economics, Industrial Economics, Agricultural Economics, World Economics, and Finance and Trade.

10. Two books were published on the Daqing Oil Company: *Daqing Gongye Qiye Guanli (Daqing's Industrial Enterprise Management)* and *Dui Daqing Jingyan de Zhengzhi Jingjixue Kaocha (A Political Economic Investigation of Daqing's Experience),* both published in Beijing in 1979.

11. Data collected during two meetings with top officials of the two associations in Beijing on July 7, 1979 and September 6, 1979. The Chinese names of the two associations were Zhongguo Guanli Xiandaihua Yanjiuhui and Zhongguo Jishu Jingji Yanjiuhui, respectively.

12. "Zhongguo Qiye Guanli Xiehui Zhangcheng" (Constitution of the China Enterprise Management Association), *Jingji Guanli (Economic Management),* March 1979.

13. The educational institutions that took part in the conference included: Hubei Agricultural

Machinery Institute, Jilin Institute of Technology, Shanxi Mechanical Engineering Institute, Hebei Electrical Engineering Institute, Beijing Institute of Economics, Tianjin Institute of Finance and Economics, Liaoning Institute of Finance and Economics, Hubei Institute of Finance and Economics, and Wuhan Steel Institute.

14. The First Ministry vice-minister responsible for personnel told me in late 1979 that his role was "to take care of a family of three million people." Did he mean three million employees, or three million employees and dependents? In the latter case, the ministry's employees might number between 750,000 and 900,000, if the size of the average urban family in China and the possibility that more than one member of the same family worked for the ministry are taken into consideration. This range is small for the size of the ministry. The interpretation of three million employees seems more plausible.

15. Data in the section on management executive training were based principally on personal notes; also *Xinhua News Agency Bulletin* of July 5, 7, and 28, 1980; August 19 and 20, 1980; December 2 and 19, 1980; March 27, 1981; June 16, 1981; August 15 and 24, 1981; September 18, 1981; November 20, 1981; and May 14, 1982; Kang Shi-en, "Yao Xia Dajuexin, Hua Daliqi, ba Qiye Guanli Gongzuo Zhuahao" ("With Great Determination and Great Effort, Grasp Enterprise Management"), *Jingji Guanli (Economic Management)*, March 1979; "Guanyu 'Gongye Jingji yu Qiye Guanli Jiben Zhishi Jianzuo' de Jige Wenti Da Duzhi" ("Answering Readers' Questions on 'Lectures on Basic Knowledge of Industrial Economics and Enterprise Management'"), *Jingji Guanli (Economic Management)*, July 1980; and "Outline Report on the National Forum on Reforming the Industrial Management System," issued jointly by the State Economic Commission and the State Council Office for the Reform of the Management System, March 14, 1981, in *Issues & Studies*, April 1982.

16. Foreign experts were full-time employees, though in a special category, of Chinese organizations for periods of months, usually a year or more. In addition to foreign experts, foreign instructors were invited to lecture in China for periods of a few weeks. They were often jointly sponsored by a Chinese organization and a foreign counterpart.

17. More than once management educators confided to me that the organizations they belonged to were interested in establishing professional contacts and exchange programs with their foreign counterparts. Yet they were at a loss as to what programs to establish and how.

18. The delegation included representatives of China's economic and management intelligentsia, scholars and industrialists. It visited the United States under the auspices of the National Committee on U.S.-China Relations, was sponsored by the schools of business of five universities—Massachusetts Institute of Technology, Harvard University, The University of Pennsylvania, Indiana University and Stanford University—and was funded in the U.S. principally from corporate sources.

19. One may speculate that those were the factions that attempted to get back to power following the height of the Cultural Revolution but did not truly succeed until after the death of Mao Ze-dong.

20. Both Ma Hong and Xue Mu-qiao, as advisors to the State Council among other positions, have played a crucial role in the formulation of recent national economic policies.

21. I am indebted to Professor Richard D. Robinson for sharing this observation with me.

22. *Meiguo Zenyang Peiyang Qiye Guanli Rencai (How the United States Trains Enterprise Management Personnel)*, (Beijing: Chinese Industrial and Commercial Executive Management Delegation, Chinese Academy of Social Sciences Press, 1980). The book was well received by the public and went through a second printing soon after its publication.

23. These materials were highly prized in China, and, for many individuals and organizations, con-

stituted their sole source of information, clearly indicating the high degree of isolation Chinese education organizations had experienced until then. The possession of original copies of such materials soon became a status symbol for many Chinese.

24. Foreign books are expensive by Chinese standards. The average price of a management book is more than half the monthly salary of a skilled worker. Typically, a Chinese organization ordered one copy per book. The China Books Import and Export Corporation provided a centralized method of purchasing foreign books, with a high degree of control. Books in high demand were often offset-printed in China from a purchased copy.

25. Chinese colleagues often told me that: "There are still people in China who say 'What do we need management education and management schools for? We have been running our country for centuries without them.'"

26. The great concern of the Chinese for the proper naming and definition of the various branches of management fits well with the concept of Rectification of Names (*zheng min*) in China's traditional intellectual history. The concept is based on the importance of order, which is created by the proper definition and description of various elements at play.

Chapter 5

1. Details of the Sino-Soviet economic cooperation and the role of the Soviet transfer of technology in China's industrialization can be found in a number of published studies. A limited selection would include the Joint Economic Committee, Congress of the United States, Studies on China, particularly those of 1967, 1972 and 1975; A. Eckstein, *Communist China's Economic Growth and Foreign Trade* (New York: McGraw-Hill, 1966); Y.L. Wu, *The Steel Industry in Communist China* (New York: Praeger, 1965); M.G. Clark, *The Development of China's Steel Industry and Soviet Technical Aid* (Ithaca, N.Y.: ILR Press, 1973); C.Y. Cheng, *The Machine Building Industry in Communist China* (New York, 1971); and F.H. Mah, *The Foreign Trade of Mainland China* (Edinburgh, 1972).

2. Many features of the Soviet management system were reintroduced with modification in Chinese enterprises after the early 1960s.

3. Interview with Bo Yi-bo, then vice-premier, in Beijing, December 1979.

4. I collected information on the state of China's computer development and industry during numerous visits to computer installations in research institutes and universities, and in discussions with computer scientists and users.

5. As an indication of the low level of standardization and quality, in some computer installations a magnetic reel originally written on one magnetic drive had to be read and written on that same drive. It could not be read on a drive of identical brand and model. Also, a computer passed quality control merely if there was no breakdown in its electronic circuitry after a certain number of hours of testing operations. The factory warranty expired following a few hours of customer use.

6. In 1978, I was told that the State Planning Commission did not use computerized input-output tables in its preparation of the national plan. Also, I learned that the Chinese customs authorities were testing a mini-computer system with a multi-user inquiry and retrieval capability.

7. For comparative purposes, in the late 1960s, IBM's training programs for data processing systems engineers consisted of about the same amount of instruction time in basically the same subjects.

8. With the rapid growth of China's foreign trade in 1978, foreign trade corporations' resources were strained to the limits. I have heard of a number of cases where trade corporations would not represent Chinese organizations to help them import goods or equipment because of lack of time and personnel.

9. Assuming that the goods to be purchased and their suppliers were readily identified, and that the commercial transactions as well as shipping went smoothly, the two-month deadline was tight but feasible. But the need to obtain export licenses, as required by United States law, made the deadline impossible to meet.

10. Following an original purchase, obtaining spare parts and accessories from abroad for the maintenance and normal operation of imported technology posed serious problems to the end-users, since it necessitated a foreign exchange allocation, which required cumbersome administrative procedure. Often, requests for such allocations were denied, particularly if they were for small installations or small parts, or if made by an organization lacking the proper connections, power or prestige. Such denials usually resulted in the inability of the end-users to operate their imported equipment efficiently, if at all, particularly if the parts could not be produced locally.

11. Foreign trade corporations held a monopoly on the conduct of China's foreign trade.

12. The original number of personnel assigned to the center in its first few months varied. The number provided represents an average.

13. These graduates were educated during the Cultural Revolution, at a time when education and academic excellence were not stressed. The Chinese did not expect high performance from such graduates.

14. The number 12 is approximate because some of the participants had other responsibilities concurrent with the second stage of their training and did not participate full time.

15. The collection and management of data in factories and other economic organizations were poor, erratic and, at times, politically and ideologically discouraged.

16. Payroll features included were: transportation subsidy, income subsidy, water fees, kitchen fees, electricity fees, rent, furniture leasing fees, gas fees, nursery school fees, meal expenses, cooperative loans and short-term advances, union fees, sick leave income adjustment, and cadre school income adjustment. The number of possible entries reflected the primary role the workplace played in the daily life of the employees.

17. I acted as a consultant to the factory for a period of over one year to help its management develop data processing production applications. The principal source of data for this section is participant observation, which took place over a number of visits lasting a few days each to the factory. Supplementary data were collected in interviews and discussions with individuals who had been closely involved in that transfer of technology.

18. It is estimated that half of the computer equipment imported in China, costing billions of U.S. dollars, is unused (see Jeremy Mark, "China Learning the Hard Way," in "A Special Report—Technology in the Workplace," *The Asian Wall Street Journal Weekly,* p. 8C, September 30, 1985).

Chapter 6

1. Lack of cooperation between universities and factories has often deserved the complaints it receives from the Chinese leadership. Yet, at the same time, two reasons might explain this lack of cooperation: the enterprise's perception of intellectuals as too theoretical, lacking an understanding of the business world, and often politically under fire. Also, operating in an economic system that is highly centralized, perceiving little incentive to take risks, and lacking the pressure of an effective accountability system, the enterprise is not pressed to look for outside consultation, help and support, including from the academic world.

2. In a separate case, members of the university's old computer center ordered and purchased from abroad newly developed microprocessor equipment for scientific applications they had in mind.

After the delivery of the equipment, they found that it did not fit their needs. It was put aside unused. It turned out that the sole source of technical information available to them for selecting the equipment was a one-sheet flyer announcing the equipment. Thousands of scarce foreign exchange dollars were thus wasted.

3. I have repeatedly heard complaints expressed by cadre in central government offices that management in subordinate organizations often got them involved in detail affairs of those organizations. The cadre attributed this situation to a lack of initiative on the part of the management. Or is it also due to management's lack of autonomy?

4. For example, both the general management and the technical management at the factory thought that the selection, development and implementation of computerized management applications, believed to be principally technical questions, lay within the responsibility of the computer center and necessitated little involvement from the factory's top leadership. The strategic implications of the computerized applications for the daily management and performance of the factory did not seem to be fully realized then.

5. For example, when it became aware that the management of the computer center was neglecting the training of the center's personnel and was reducing the service to the users, the university leadership had little effective leverage to modify the situation.

6. The Jade Buddha Temple, located in Shanghai, houses a most exquisite Buddha statue carved out of white jade. The valuable computer, like that statue, was housed and protected in the computer center. My many requests that trainees' access to the equipment be facilitated went unheeded. Only when I mentioned the ''Jade Buddha Temple'' syndrome were communication channels cleared, resulting in limited positive actions. The power of cultural communication!

7. I was hired in 1978 on an experimental basis, the first foreigner to work in China in systems engineering and management since the Sino-Soviet Rift in 1960. Subsequently, the Chinese have employed scores of other professionals in these fields.

Chapter 7

1. The industrial ministry's national plans for the development of management academic programs and cadre training programs were revised downward a number of times in 1979 and 1980. Whereas the original plans reflected the pressing needs for the development of management resources and skills, it seems that an underestimation of the tasks at hand (reflecting a lack of experience in the field) and the constant shortage of resources (due mainly to the lower priority assigned to those tasks by the highest level of the ministry's leadership) were two determining factors in the downward revision of the plans.

2. Such an argument was often used; it was one of the few kinds of leverage an organization had over the center.

3. The poor results of the first stage of the course compared to the excellent ones of the second won that argument for the university.

Bibliography

"A Boom-to-Bust TV Saga." *China Business Review* (Washington) (July-August 1981).

Agar, M.H. *The Professional Stranger: An Informal Introduction to Ethnography.* New York: Academic Press, 1980.

Andors, S. *China's Industrial Revolution.* Armonk, N.Y.: M.E. Sharpe, 1977.

Battat, Joseph Y. Unpublished Newsletters. Hanover, N.H.: Institute of Current World Affairs, 1980-81.

Berney, K. "China's Labor System." *The China Business Review* (Washington) 8, no. 5 (September-October 1981).

Brugger, W. *Democracy and Organization in the Chinese Industrial Enterprise, 1948-53.* Cambridge, 1976.

Byrd, William. *China's Financial System: The Changing Role of Banks.* Boulder, Colo.: Westview Press, 1983.

Byrd, William, et al. *Recent Chinese Economic Reforms: Studies of Two Industrial Enterprises.* Washington, D.C., 1984.

China Policy for the Next Decade: Report of the Atlantic Council's Committee on China Policy. Cambridge, Mass: Oelgeschlager, Gunn & Hain, 1984.

Chu, D.S.K., ed. *Sociology and Society in Contemporary China, 1979-83.* Armonk, N.Y.: M.E. Sharpe, 1984.

Clark, M. Gardner. *The Development of China's Steel Industry and Soviet Technical Aid.* Ithaca, N.Y.: ILR Press, 1973.

Cohen, R., L.L. Laugness, J. Middleton, V.C. Uchendu, and J.W. VanStone. "Entree into the Field." In *A Handbook of Method of Cultural Anthropology,* edited by R. Naroll and R. Cohen. Garden City, N.Y.: Natural History Press, 1970.

Congress of the United States. Joint Economic Committee. *China: A Reassessment of the Economy.* Washington, D.C., 1975.

_____. *China under the Four Modernizations.* Washington, D.C., 1982.

_____. *Chinese Economy Post-Mao.* Washington, D.C., 1978.

_____. *An Economic Profile of Mainland China.* Washington, D.C., 1967.

_____. *People's Republic of China: An Economic Assessment.* Washington, D.C., 1972.

Crane, J.G. and M.V. Angrosino. *Field Projects in Anthropology: A Student Handbook.* Morristown, N.J.: Waveland Press, 1974.

Daqing Gongye Qiye Guanli (Daqing's Industrial Enterprise Management). Beijing, 1979.

Documents of the First Session of the Fifth National People's Congress of the People's Republic of China. Beijing, 1976.

Donnithorne, A. *China's Economic System.* London: Praeger, 1967.

Dui Daqing Jingyan de Zhengshi Jingjixue Kaocha (A Political Economic Investigation of Daqing's Experience). Beijing, 1979.

Eckstein, A. *Communist China's Economic Growth and Foreign Trade.* New York: McGraw-Hill, 1966.

_____. *China's Economic Revolution.* Cambridge; New York: Cambridge University Press, 1977.

Editorial. "Zhengque Renshi Xin de Bazi Fangzhen" (Correctly Understand the New Eight-Character Policy). *Jingji Guangli (Economic Management)* Beijing, no. 6, 1979.

Farmer, R.N. and B. Richman. *Comparative Management and Economic Progress.* Homewood, Ill.: R.D. Irwin, 1965.

Ge-ping, Q., and L. Wo-yen, eds. *Managing the Environment in China.* Dublin: Tycooly International Publishing Ltd., 1984.

Gongye Jingying Guanli Jingyan Xuanbian—1981 (Selections on Industrial Management Experiences 1981). Beijing, 1981.

Griffin, K., ed. *Institutional Reform and Economic Development in the Chinese Countryside.* Armonk, N.Y.: M.E. Sharpe, 1984.

Gu Zong-chang. "Guanyu Guoying Qiye Zifuyunkui de Jige Wenti" (Problems in State-Owned Enterprises' Responsibility for Profits and Losses). *Jingji Guanli (Economic Management).* Beijing, July 1980.

Hebei University Economics Department. *Gongye Qiye Guanli (Industrial Enterprise Management).* Baoding, Hebei, 1977.

Ho, A.K. *Developing the Economy of the People's Republic of China.* New York: Praeger, 1982.

Hu Qiao-mu. "Act in Accordance with Economic Laws, Step Up the Four Modernizations." *Xinhua News Agency Bulletin.* Beijing, October 5, 1978.

Huan Xiang. "Cong Guanli Dao Jingli" ("From Bureaucrat to Manager"). *Jingji Guanli (Economic Management).* Beijing, November 1980.

Jing Feng. "Quanmin Suoyoushi Qiye Shixing Zifuyunkui Shi Ge Hao Banfa" ("To Implement [the System of] Responsibility for Profits and Losses in Enterprises Owned by the Whole People Is a Good Measure"). *Jingji Guanli (Economic Management).* Beijing, no. 9, 1979.

Kan Shi-en. "Yao Xia Dajuexin, Hua Daliqi, Ba Qiye Guanli Gongzuo Zhuahao" ("With Great Determination and Great Effort, Grasp Enterprises Management"). *Jingji Guanli (Economic Management).* Beijing, March 1979.

Klenner, W. *The Chinese Economy: Structure and Reform in the Domestic Economy and in Foreign Trade.* Hamburg: Verlag Weltarchiv, 1982.

Lardy, N.R. *Agriculture in China's Modern Economic Development.* Cambridge; New York: Cambridge University Press, 1983.

Leng, Shao-chuan. "The Chinese Judicial System: A New Direction." In *Organizational Behavior in Chinese Society,* edited by S.L. Greenblatt, R.W. Wilson, and A.A. Wilson. New York: Praeger, 1981.

Lin Ling. "Sichuansheng Yinianlai Kuoda Qiye Zizhuguan de Shidian Qingkuang" ("The Situation of Sichuan Province's Experiment in Expanding the Enterprise Right for Self-Management in the Last Year") *Jingji Guanli (Economic Management).* Beijing, June 1980.

———. "Sichuansheng Liangnianlai Jingji Tizhi Gaige de Jingyan yu Wenti" ("Experiences and Problems of the Reform of the Economic System of Sichuan Province in the Last Two Years"). *Jingji Guanli (Economic Management).* Beijing, June 1981.

Luo Jing-fen. "Quanmin Suoyoushi Qiye Keyi Shixing Zifuyunkui" ("Enterprises Owned by the Whole People May Implement [the System of] Responsibility for Profits and Losses"). *Jingji Guanli (Economic Management).* Beijing, no. 6, 1979.

Ma Hong, ed. *Zhongguo Shehuizhuyi Guoying Gongye Qiye Guanli (China's Socialist State-Owned Industrial Enterprise Management).* Second edition. Beijing, 1980.

Ma Quan-shan, et al. "Zai Wenbu Fazhanzhong Zhubu Wanshan Gongye Jingji Zerenzhi" ("Gradually Perfect the System of Industrial Economic Responsibility in the Course of Steady Development"). *Jingji Yanjiu (Economic Studies).* Beijing, no. 2, 1982.

Malinowski, B. *Argonauts of the Western Pacific.* London: G. Routledge, 1922.

Mao Ze-dong. *Selected Works of Mao Ze-dong.* Five volumes. Beijing, 1965, 1967, 1969, and 1977.

Marx, Karl. "The Critique of the Gotha Program." In *Basic Writings on Politics and Philosophy by Karl Marx and Friedrich Engels,* edited by Lewis S. Feuer. Garden City, N.Y.: Doubleday, 1959.

Meiguo Zengyang Peiyang Qiye Guanli Rencai (How the United States Trains Enterprise Manage-ment Personnel). Chinese Industrial and Commercial Executive Management Delegation. Beijing, 1980.

Nash, D. "The Ethnologist as Stranger." *Southwestern Journal of Anthropology* 19 (1963): 149-67.

"On Questions of Party History." *Beijing Review* 24, no. 27 (July 1981).

"Outline Report on the National Forum on Reforming the Industrial Management System." Issued jointly by the State Economic Commission and the State Council Office for the Reform of the Management System. March 14, 1981. In *Issues and Studies.* Taipei, April 1982.

People's University. Industrial Economics Department. *Zhongguo Shehuizhuyi Gongye Qiye Guanli (China's Socialist Industrial Enterprise Management).* Beijing, 1980.

Perkins, D.H. *China's Modern Economy in Historical Perspective.* Stanford, Calif.: Stanford University Press, 1975.

————. *Market Control and Planning in Communist China.* Cambridge, Mass.: Harvard University Press, 1966.

"Personal Income in China." *The China Business Review* (Washington) 8, no. 2 (March-April 1981).

Ren Tao. "Sichuan Baige Shidian Qiye Sijian Chengjiao de Yuanyin Hezai?" ("What Are the Reasons for the Rapid Success of Sichuan Province's 100 Experimental Enterprises?"). *Jingji Guanli (Economic Management).* Beijing, December 1979.

Richman, B.M. *Industrial Society in Communist China.* New York: Random House, 1969.

Robinson, J. *Economic Management in China.* London: Anglo-Chinese Educational Institute, 1975.

Schell, O. *To Get Rich Is Glorious: China in the '80s.* New York: Pantheon, 1984.

Schram, S.R., ed. *Authority, Participation, and Cultural Change in China.* Cambridge: Cambridge University Press, 1973.

Schurmann, Franz. *Ideology and Organization in Communist China.* Berkeley, Calif.: University of California Press, 1968.

Shanghai Finance and Economics Institute, Shanghai Branch, Shanghai Academy of Social Sciences. *Shehuizhuyi Gongye Qiye Guanli (Socialist Industrial Enterprise Management).* Shanghai, 1980.

Shi Zheng-wen. "Readjusting the National Economy: Why and How?" *Beijing Review* 22, no. 26 (June 1979).

Solinger, D.J. *Chinese Business under Socialism: The Politics of Domestic Commerce, 1949-80.* Berkeley, Calif.: University of California Press, 1984.

Spradley, J.P. *The Ethnographic Interview.* New York: Holt, Rinehart and Winston, 1979.

"Style of Work." *Beijing Review.* 24, no. 44 (November 1981).

Teiwes, F.C. *Leadership, Legitimacy, and Conflict in China: From a Charismatic Mao to the Politics of Succession.* Armonk, N.Y.: M.E. Sharpe, 1984.

Tian Yun. "More Authority for Enterprises Revives the Economy." *Beijing Review* 24, no. 14 (April 1981).

"Vice-Premier Bo Yibo on China's Current Priorities." *The China Business Review* (Washington) 7, no. 6 (November-December 1980).

Vidich, A.J. "Participant Observer and the Collection and Interpretation of Data." In *Qualitative Methodology,* edited by Wm. J. Filstead. Chicago: Markham Publishing Company, 1970.

Weida de Shinian (Ten Great Years). Beijing, 1959.

Wood, A. *Economic Evaluation of Investment Projects: Possibilities and Problems of Applying Western Methods in China.* Washington: World Bank, 1984.

World Bank. *China: Socialist Economic Development—The Main Report.* Report No. 3391-CHA. Washington, D.C., 1981.

Wu Kai-tai. "Quanmin Suoyouzhi Qiye Bu Neng Shixing Zifuyunkui" ("Enterprises Owned by the Whole People Cannot Implement [the System of] Responsibility for Profits and Losses"). *Jingji Guanli (Economic Management).* Beijing, no. 9, 1979.

Wu, Y.L. *The Steel Industry in Communist China.* New York: Praeger, 1965.

Xia Zhen. "A New Strategy for Economic Development." *Beijing Review* 24, no. 32 (August 1981).

Xu Zhi-fan and Zhou Jing-hua. "Economic Policies in Rural Areas." *Beijing Review* 22, no. 16 (April 1979).

Xue Mu-qiao. *Dangqian Woguo Jingji Ruogan Wenti (Certain Current Problems in Our National Economy.* Beijing, 1980.

———. "More on Economic Reform." *Beijing Review* 23, no. 36, (September 1981).

Xue Mu-qiao, et al. *The Socialist Transformation of the National Economy in China.* Beijing, 1960.

Zhang Shu-guang. "Reform the Economic Structure and Increase the Macroeconomic Results." *Social Science in China.* Beijing, no. 1, 1982.

Zhao Yu-shen. "Current Economic Situation on the Chinese Main-Land." *Issues and Studies* (Taipei) 17, no. 10 (October 1981).

"Zhongguo Qiye Guanli Xiehui Zhangcheng" ("Constitution of the China Enterprise Management Association"). *Jingji Guanli (Economic Management).* Beijing, March 1979.

Zhou Zhun-hua, "Lun Woguo Shehuizhuyi Gongyouzhi de Zhudao Diwei yu Gaige Tujing" ("On the Leading Position of, and Ways of Reforming, Our Socialist Public Ownership"). *Jingji Kexue (Economic Science).* Beijing, no. 1, 1982.

Periodicals

Beijing Review, Beijing.

Issues & Studies, Taipei.

Jingji Daobao (Economic Reporter), Beijing.

Jingji Guanli (Economic Management), Beijing.

Jingji Kexue (Economic Science), Beijing.

Jingji Yanjiu (Economic Studies), Beijing.

Shehui Kexue (Social Sciences), Shanghai.

Social Science in China (in English), Beijing.

The Australian Journal of Chinese Affairs, Canberra.

The China Business Review, Washington.

The New York Times, New York.

Xinhua News Agency Bulletin, Beijing.

Zhongguo Jingji Nianjian (Almanac of China's Economy), Beijing.

Zhongguo Shehui Kexue (Social Science in China), Beijing.

Index